Managing Improving Primary Schools

Managing Improving Primary Schools:
Using Evidence-based Management and Leadership

Geoff Southworth and Colin Conner

UK   Falmer Press, 11 New Fetter Lane, London, EC4P 4EE

USA   Falmer Press, Routledge Inc, 29 West 35th Street, New York, NY10001

First published in 1999

A catalogue record for this book is available from the British Library

ISBN   0 7507 0834 4 cased
ISBN   0 7507 0833 6 paper

Library of Congress Cataloging-in-Publication Data are available on request

Jacket design by Caroline Archer

Typeset in 11/13pt by Garamond
Graphicraft Limited, Hong Kong

Printed in Great Britain by Biddles Ltd., Guildford and King's Lynn on paper which has a specified pH value on final paper manufacture of not less than 7.5 and is therefore 'acid free'.

Every effort has been made to contact copyright holders for their permission to reprint material in this book. The publishers would be grateful to hear from any copyright holder who is not here acknowledged and will undertake to rectify any errors or omissions in future editions of this book.

Contents

Acknowledgments

There are many teachers who have worked with us on courses in Cambridge and Reading and teachers and headteachers in schools who have joined us in our research activities that have helped to formulate the ideas discussed in this publication. To them we offer our thanks and hope that we have fairly represented their ideas and reactions.

We would also like to thank the following for permission to reproduce extracts from copyright material.

Sylva, K., Roy, C. and Painter, M. for an extract from *Childwatching at Playgroup and Nursery School* (1980), published by McIntyre. John Elliott for an illustration from the *Ford Teaching Project* materials. Routledge Publishers for permission to reproduce the observation categories of the pupil and teacher records used in the Oracle Project and published in Galton, M., Simon, B. and Croll, P. (eds) (1980) *Inside the Primary Classroom*, pp. 12, 13 and 17. David Hopkins for allowing us to reproduce Figure 8.2 from his book *A Teacher's Guide to Classroom Research* (1993, 2nd Edition), published by Open University Press. The National Union of Teachers for permission to reproduce questionnaires from their publication *Schools Speak for Themselves: Towards a Framework for Self-Evaluation* (1997) by MacBeath, J., Boyd, B., Rand, J. and Bell, S. David Hargreaves for permission to include an extract from *Mapping Change in Schools. The Cambridge Manual of Research Techniques* (1994), by Ainscow, M., Hargreaves, D., Hopkins, D., Balshaw, M. and Black-Hawkins, K. Addison-Wesley/Longman for permission to reproduce an amended version of page 110 from Acheson, K. and Gall, M. (1980) *Techniques in the Clinical Supervision of Teachers.* Kendall/Hunt Publishing Company for permission to include an extract from *Classroom Supervision and Instructional Improvement: A Synergetic Process* by Bellon, J. J. et al. (1980). Essex LEA for permission to reproduce extracts from the Learning Perception Survey. Birmingham LEA for Figure 1.1. Finally, we would like to offer a grateful thanks to Peter Dudley for permission to draw upon his work in the final two illustrations of the ideas described in this publication.

List of Figures and Tables

Introduction

This book aims to support teachers and headteachers who wish to develop an evidence-based approach to their work and their schools' successes. Now that self-managing schools have become established in England and Wales, the next phase of development involves encouraging all schools to be self-improving organizations and to achieve this staff in schools need to conduct school self-evaluation.

While self-evaluation has been common for many years, today it is being promoted in a more focused manner. Whereas self-evaluation was once more concerned with process issues, today the emphasis is on both processes and outcomes.

Self-evaluation relies on the collection of reliable information that can be used to inform decisions and priorities for improvement efforts. Monitoring teaching and learning, auditing pupils' progress, reviewing patterns and trends in the school and the pupils' achievements all play a part in self-evaluation. While at a general level all teachers are aware of this, what many, in our experience, are less aware of are the techniques and strategies they might use to collect valid information. This book offers ways of doing this.

This first part of the book makes the case for using an evidence-based approach to school management and leadership. An overview of recent developments in school improvement and self-evaluation is set out, alongside the need to build capacity in the school to support and sustain school improvement. Moreover, we argue that there is an increasing emphasis being placed on schools to concentrate on and evaluate the quality of teaching. Hence, an evidence-based approach to classroom practice – to teaching and learning – is now central to school improvement.

Throughout the discussion examples of how headteachers and senior staff in schools with whom we have worked are included to illustrate the ideas we raise and to show that what we have to say is already happening in some schools.

Part 2 describes the techniques staff can use to collect evidence. We describe many approaches under five headings: observation; interviewing; questionnaires; analysing documents; analysing assessment information. The section is characterized throughout by illustration and examples so that readers can see how others have used these approaches. This section is intended to be practical. We hope readers will draw directly on the ideas set out here and use them to conduct their own school-based enquiries, as we know many other teachers have done.

Part 3 builds on Part 2, since we set out our ideas for managing the use of evidence in schools. We report on what we have discovered about teachers' reactions to data and argue that staff must be well prepared to handle data if negative responses are to be avoided. We then go on to make a case for starting with and using pupil perception data. Primary school children's perceptions of learning are formative in shaping their achievements, thus it follows that it is important to take such perceptions into account on a regular, systematic basis. Moreover, experience shows that this information is of great interest to teachers and other members of staff. Pupils' perceptions can make a useful starting point in using data. Then we move on to present four case examples of an evidence-based approach in action. These examples include: how a school used school-based enquiry to follow-up an Ofsted inspection of the school; how a primary head examined the school's internal capacity to improve and worked on developing shared leadership; a school's efforts to monitor the quality of teaching and develop greater consistency among the teaching staff; and managing school-based enquiry using a combination of audit, review, staff development time and pupils' assessment data to establish an evidence-based approach to school improvement.

In the Conclusion we briefly summarize Parts 1, 2 and 3 and suggest that when schools fully implement and establish an evidence-based approach to school improvement then a particular school culture develops. This culture is one where staff work and learn together. There is peer observation, peer support and mutual learning. In particular, there is a concerted effort to develop teachers' pedagogy. Teachers share their craft knowledge and understandings with one another and through mentoring, appraisal and coaching they teach one another. Such schools therefore resemble learning organizations. However, given the emphasis on pedagogy, these schools might be better described as *teaching and learning schools.*

Throughout the book we draw extensively on our work with teachers and headteachers. Where we can, we have used our knowledge of existing practice to inform our ideas. Everything we suggest in this book has been used by teachers somewhere. In other words, all of the ideas reported here have been tested and shown to be useful to staff in schools.

Essentially, an evidence-based approach to management and leadership enables headteachers, senior staff and teachers to 'learn their ways forward'. It means looking at what is already happening in the school, from a variety of standpoints (including the pupils', parents' and governors' perspectives), understanding what this means for the school's success and development and determining the next course of action.

1　The Case for Evidence-based Management and Leadership

Initiatives, changes and mandates in education keep on coming. External reforms have become the norm in education. Yet, schools are also encouraged to be self-managing institutions. These two trends do not always sit easily alongside one another. Self-determining schools find the prescriptions of others difficult to accept, let alone implement. Or, expressed another way: How can we manage ourselves when others keep on setting the agenda? One resolution of this duality, and one which prevents it becoming a dilemma, is to understand that self-managing schools need to be organizations that are constantly aware of their external environments and their internal achievements and always striving to balance the two. Sometimes the external factors will weigh more heavily than internal ones; at another time the point of balance will shift towards internal conditions. However, if the point of balance is dynamic, then what will help staff understand where the fulcrum needs to be placed at any one time is a keen sense of evaluation and school review.

The case for an evidence-based approach to school management, leadership and improvement relies on school self-evaluation. For example, when the Department for Education and Employment (DfEE) introduced target-setting, one of the guidance documents despatched to all schools stated that target-setting aids school review. Pupil performance targets provide firm measures against which to judge recent progress because headteachers, teachers and governing bodies can see more clearly whether they are achieving or falling short in their main goals (DfEE, 1997b, p. 8). At the same time, school reviews should help staff in schools to identify the approaches to improvement which work. From an examination of whether set targets have been met, senior staff should be able to see which strategies and tactics adopted by staff have contributed in a major way to accomplishing these goals. In other words, target-setting has to be based on self-enquiry, audit, review and evaluation, as the DfEE advisers were themselves keenly aware:

> Target-setting alone will not raise standards in schools. They [targets] are the next step in improving development planning. They need to fit

into a sensible cycle of school review, planning and action. (DfEE, 1997b, p. 8)

This represents our position too. At the heart of the self-managing and self-improving school lies school self-evaluation.

A cycle of review, planning and action is something we have been committed to for many years. We have long seen school development as cyclical and revolving around 'what are essentially evaluation processes within which a repertoire of evaluation techniques can be utilised' (Holly and Southworth, 1989, p. 2). In turn, this outlook was based on four questions:

What do we need to look at?
Where are we now?
Where do we want to be?
How do we get there?

These questions equate with the identification of priority needs for development, stocktaking of current practice in chosen areas of focus, target-setting and strategic planning in terms of an action plan prior to implementation (p. 45).

Clearly, school self-evaluation is not a new idea. It has been around for more than 20 years. Since the original ideas were developed in the 1970s and 1980s there has been much valuable experience gained. Also, following the structural education reforms of the late 1980s we have seen the concept and the principles of procedure of school review begin to flower in newly variegated ways. The target-setting initiative is just one manifestation of this new blossoming. Another is the introduction of self-managing schools.

Schools may now be more self-managing and self-determining than formerly, and certainly schools today enjoy greater institutional autonomy than a decade ago, yet their autonomy is largely only from local government authority – the LEAs (local education authorities), but not from central government's authority and control. Hence, although schools enjoy greater levels of freedom, they are also required to be more accountable than ever before. Autonomy in England and Wales has been accompanied by a corresponding increase in the exercise of public accountability. The most tangible form of accountability is the inspection of all schools by a team of inspectors external to the school. These teams are accredited and contracted by the Office for Standards in Education (Ofsted), a government agency. While it is right and proper that schools be held to account, the danger with the Ofsted style of inspection, where every school is now visited once every six years, is that staff become dependent upon the inspectors' audit and wait for them to tell the school what to focus on next. In other words, while schools may have become independent of LEAs, some may become more dependent upon the Ofsted analyses of the schools' work.

We do not approve of such a passive approach to improvement or review. Rather, in line with almost all the teachers and schools we work with, we believe in using evaluation techniques and cycles of review to better understand one's own progress and that of the pupils' perform-ance. It is for these reasons that this book has been put together. We want to offer colleagues the tools of evaluation, within the principles and parameters of school self-evaluation.

Perhaps one test of whether your school is a self-evaluating and self-improving school is to play the 'envelope game'. This 'game' involves staff identifying their school's strengths and weaknesses prior to the school being inspected. A reasonably full audit should be made, drawing upon the school's development plan, action plan, pupil tar-gets, success in meeting the targets, pupils' learning data and school performance information, as well as detailed reviews of the school's organizational units (e.g. key stage units, year groups, subject areas). From an analysis of these data the specific areas of success and concern could be noted, recorded and put into an envelope. When the inspectors visit, observe the learning and teaching in the school and produce their inspection report, the contents of the envelope might then be com-pared with the inspectors' main findings and key issues. Ideally, any comparison between the two should develop a dialogue not only about the validity of each group's perception, but also the veracity of their judgments. Some interesting discussion could develop which might enhance both the quality of school self-review and the detail and scope of the inspectors' insights.

If the Ofsted programme of school inspections is one reason why school self-evaluation has today changed from how it was conceptual-ized a decade or more ago, another significant development has been the introduction of benchmarking. Today, truly evaluatory schools do not only examine their own levels of performance; they also contrast these with the success of other schools in their LEA and with schools in similar circumstances. This is consistent with the idea that evaluation is a 'spanning activity' (Holly and Southworth, 1989, p. 2), although today it is a far more comparative form of review than anything envis-aged 10 to 15 years ago. Consequently, the four questions of school self-evaluation which were originally advocated have now been extended by a fifth:

How do we compare with similar schools?

This question looks not only at how well a school is doing, but how well it *should* be doing by comparing current and previous results with those of similar schools. (DfEE, 1997, p. 7)

Such a question clearly extends the scope of awareness staff in any school will have of their individual and school performance. It moves them from a narrow relativism, when staff might have seen their work only in reference to previous years' efforts, to a wider appreciation of the school's achievements. It also enables staff to look more deeply. For example, from our work with schools we know that by using comparative data staff have been aware that although their schools have been making progress, relative to some other schools, these rates of progress have looked modest and this has stimulated senior staff to set more challenging targets within shorter timescales and to accelerate the pace of improvement.

Wider awareness and deeper analysis provide the foundations of an evidence-based approach to school management, leadership and improvement. This approach marks a significant forward movement in school self-evaluation because it encompasses both the analyses of process issues and outcome indicators. It looks at the school's internal performance levels and at how these compare with other schools. It draws upon inspection information, LEA data and teachers' professional judgments. Moreover, the data collection and analysis is undertaken with a commitment to improve the school's performance over time and to enhance pupils' learning and development.

There are numerous signs of this evidence-based approach being applied systematically in schools today. Recent visits we have made to research schools' approaches to value-added analyses of the pupils' learning show how some heads and deputies or assistant heads are using data sets to develop understandings and diagnose issues and priorities. Several heads we know are now using staff development days to review these data and to develop interpretations of them and to understand their implications for the school and its improvement priorities.

It should not be presumed from the foregoing that all of this means becoming obsessed with pupil test scores. One school we know has looked at the quality of school outcomes in the broadest sense and ranges across curriculum, pastoral and management areas. The head-teacher is aware there is much scope 'for in-house value added invest-igations' and that schools should be encouraged to 'get to grips with other evidence – often internal and sometimes informal – to cast light on a range of outcomes that extend well beyond SATs (Pfister, 1997, p. 22).

The questions staff often ask themselves and the data they use to address them include the following:

Communication *How effectively have we created two way channels to foster shared understandings with pupils and parents?*

Data could be derived from: the nature of parents' letters to schools; parent attendance at (and response to) curriculum and consultation meetings; yearly questionnaires; homework record book comments; pupil attendance and late records; response to standard letters; feedback forms in the home/school information pack; parent response slips from reports; teachers' marking comments; pupil comments as drafting and writing partners. Lack of data is also data! No complaints about bullying or no holiday absence may indicate that communication at both child and adult level is ineffective. No response slips returned may mean something else.

Engagement *Are things being accomplished at home and at school in practice as well as in policy?*

Data could be derived from any sampling undertaken by the head and subject managers as part of the school's monitoring timetable (regular) or in response to School Development Planning success criteria (*ad hoc*). Three children across the range of ability in every class, in person or through their work, can give an instant picture of the progress of referencing skills, the acquisition of [number] tables, the nature of individual targets or how often they are being heard to read at home.

Achievement and attainment *Are we seeing the progress and standards that evidence improvement?*

Data could be derived from spelling or reading ages plotted twice yearly for each year group and analysed both for longitudinal attainment (percentages of children at or near their chronological reading age, six months to a year above or below) and progress (percentages of children making less or more than six months, or one year's progress within the year). This information can then be analysed to address the quality of provision for children of different abilities (boys, girls, bilingual learners etc.) through the school; it casts light on peaks and troughs of learning at different times and in different classes. (Pfister, 1997, pp. 24–25)

What this headteacher describes here is an evidence-based approach to school management and leadership. It is clear she is able to raise these questions with her colleagues and later return to these concerns with data and indicators that show whether there is something which needs to be further examined, applauded or improved. In short: 'Monitoring widely and *making use* of the information is central to school improvement' (p. 22). Evidence illuminates the focus for a school's improvement efforts and the analysis leads to new actions. This latter point is very important. Monitoring and evaluation are key processes. This book will make this point many times over. However, evaluation is but the prelude to action.

While this point is obviously important, our experience tells us that it needs to be emphasized because one of the pitfalls of evaluation is that analysis of data does not lead to action. Rather, what sometimes happens is that analysis leads to paralysis. Some staff groups drown in all the data they collect. They keep on collecting data but never believe they have enough to answer conclusively the questions they generate. Others enjoy creating graphs and charts and see the collation of data as an end in itself. Neither of these two approaches is satisfactory. For sure, teachers need some data, but not so much that it becomes unwieldy or so time-consuming that other activities are sidelined.

The other point to highlight from Pfister's work is her idea that using evidence is central to school improvement. Such an outlook is vital to the case for an evidence-based approach to management and leadership. The whole point of conducting school reviews is to strengthen the school's work and better serve the pupils, while, at the same time, identifying effective teaching and learning and celebrating them. When this occurs then the developing or moving school becomes the improving school: that is, a school which is not just changing and keeping up to date with the latest mandate, but one which can articulate where it wants to be and can describe the journey that has been embarked on. Staff, and not just senior staff, will be able to explain the targets and objectives they have set for the pupils and themselves and will be able to describe their starting points, the pathways followed and outline the progress made. In time, the staff will also be able to call up data that shows how well they are working towards their goals and suggest what else needs to be explored and charted. These are plainly not 'strolling' schools, nor ones which simply travel hopefully. They are schools which are mapping their processes of change. They have planned and set out their journeys of improvement and are recording what they have experienced, discovered and learned as they have progressed towards their destinations.

Improving Schools

The case for an evidence-based approach to management and leadership has now been presented in outline. At the same time, some key ideas have been briefly touched on. These include:

- monitoring
- analysis
- an orientation to action
- looking closely at performance inside the school
- comparing your progress with similar schools
- target-setting
- improving the school.

While all of these ideas are closely related to each other, the idea of improving the school is the one which underpins all of them and gives both point and purpose to them.

However, one of the things we have learned over the last decade is that in order for schools to develop, each has to create and sustain the conditions for school improvement.

> Research into effective school improvement (e.g. Ainscow et al., 1994; Fullan, 1993; Stoll, 1994; West and Hopkins, 1996) emphasises the need to make sure that efforts to raise standards of achievement are accompanied by a comparable drive to build the capacity of the school as a whole to manage change. The focus on the classroom practice must be located within a planning framework which enables the school to keep on moving forward. Interventions in teaching and learning are essential but on their own will not result in sustainable improvements in levels of achievement. They need to be set within a cycle of audit, benchmarking, target setting, action planning, monitoring and evaluation which at every stage is built on the collection, analysis and use of empirical evidence. (Birmingham LEA, 1997, p. 7)

This statement both supports all that has been argued so far in this chapter and advances it. The idea that each school has to develop the internal capacity to manage change and improvement is the key step forward. School improvement has to be seen and understood as part of educational change.

Probably one of the most influential writers about the process of change in education is Michael Fullan. His book *The New Meaning of Educational Change*, published in 1991, is required reading for all students of change. The title is significant because it emphasizes some fundamental principles for understanding the effective introduction of anything new. That is, that those involved need to understand the **why**, the **what** and the **how** of any proposed innovation. Fullan identified three important stages through which any effective change progresses: **initiation**, **implementation** and **institutionalization**.

The initiation stage includes what happens in preparation for the decision to introduce anything new. For this to be effective, he suggests that participants need to understand why a change is being proposed, to see its relevance. There also has to be opportunity for participants to get ready for the change through advice, support and training and finally that there should be the provision of appropriate resources, one of the most important of which is time.

The implementation stage is often the least well prepared for because it is assumed that if you've got the first stage right, everything else falls into place and happens naturally and spontaneously. This could not be further from the truth. Fullan argues that implementation has to be carefully prepared for and, if possible, potential problems identified before they occur, with strategies established to resolve difficulties amicably and effectively. For this stage to be effective, responsibilities have to be clearly defined, there should be regular opportunities for review and there needs to be a combination of subtle pressure as well as support. By implication, sustained staff development throughout the introductory phases is essential. If this happens, Fullan believes the final stage is more likely to occur.

Institutionalization is when the initial idea becomes an automatic and established part of practice. Fullan suggests that this is achieved through the skill, commitment and broad support of teachers across the school, the continued commitment of the headteacher, the removal of competing priorities, and the availability of continuing advice and regular evaluation to learn from the collective experience.

Stoll and Fink (1996) draw upon the work of Fullan and others to produce a list of some of the central characteristics of the change process:

- There is never one and only one version of what the change should be. It is important for everyone involved to be able to share their experience and understanding and as a result to develop and change the initial proposals if experience suggests that this is appropriate.
- People need to understand the proposals and to work out their own meaning. Changes in teachers' behaviour are more likely to occur before changes in their beliefs.

- Change is a highly personal experience and for adults, as well as for children, learning is as much an emotional activity as it is a cognitive one.
- Change is approached differently in different contexts. Innovations need to be sufficiently flexible for schools to adapt them to their own circumstances and situations.
- Conflict and disagreement are inevitable. This is natural and if it isn't occurring, Huberman and Miles (1984) suggest it is likely that not much is happening.
- A combination of pressure and support is necessary. All of us need help and encouragement when learning something new and a little push on occasions to make sure that it happens.
- Change rarely involves singular acts. It is often the case that a number of different things will be happening at the same time. Sarason (1990) describes this as a 'rippling effect'; changing something in one way leads to changes elsewhere.
- Effective change takes time, therefore persistence is essential. It has been argued that even small-scale change can take between three and five years, whilst more complex restructuring may take much longer.
- A school cannot always be developing otherwise it runs out of steam. This suggests an important role for school leaders, i.e. the change process has to be managed and controlling overload is essential.
- There are many valid reasons why change does not take place. It is not just resistance on the part of more recalcitrant colleagues.
- It is not realistic to expect everyone to change. There are often perfectly justifiable reasons why some teachers are unable to adopt to a proposal, often because of lack of knowledge or experience.

School improvers need always to keep these ideas in mind. However, they also need, as acknowledged above in the quotation from Birmingham LEA, to build capacity in the school to support and sustain improvement efforts. The idea of capacity building and creating the conditions to support school improvement originates from the Improving the Quality of Education for All (IQEA) project (*see* Ainscow, Hopkins, et al., 1994). The IQEA project team worked with many primary, secondary and special schools in England. At the same time, as staff in the schools planned and implemented their specific school improvement efforts, IQEA team members also helped the staff to adapt and develop six internal conditions which enable improvement efforts to be successfully implemented. Staff were encouraged to diagnose their internal conditions in relation to their chosen change before they began their development work. The following list of the six conditions that the team members have articulated represents their 'best estimate, rather than a definitive statement, of what the important conditions are at present'. Broadly stated the six conditions are:

1   proper attention to the benefits of *enquiry and reflection*
2   a commitment to *collaborative planning*
3   the *involvement* of staff, pupils and the community in school policies and decisions
4   a commitment to *staff development*
5   effective *coordination* strategies
6   effective *leadership*, but not just of the head; the leadership function is spread throughout the school. (Ainscow, Hopkins, et al., 1994, p. 11)

These six conditions are not listed in any priority order. What is important is for staff in schools to develop all of them if they are to create and sustain the internal capacity to successfully implement and realize their improvement targets. To provide a clearer picture of these conditions we shall now briefly review them, drawing upon the ideas of Ainscow, Hopkins, Southworth and West (1994), who have not only described these six conditions in some detail, but also devised staff development activities to help teacher groups create these conditions in their schools:

Enquiry and Reflection

Schools which recognize that enquiry and reflection are important processes in school improvement find it easier to sustain improvement effort around established priorities and are better placed to monitor the extent to which policies and plans actually deliver the intended outcomes for pupils. Such enquiry and reflection involves systematic collection, interpretation, and use of school-generated data in decision-making. Also, effective strategies for reviewing the progress and impact of school policies and initiatives are needed which should include the widespread involvement of staff in the processes of data collection and analysis. It is also important that each school establishes clear ground-rules for the collection, control and use of school-based data.

Collaborative Planning

Planning for development is an essential part of the school improvement process. Planning is enriched when staff draw upon the data produced by enquiry and reflection activities and when the planning process involves as many members of staff and other groups (e.g. governors) as possible. It is also important to avoid seeing the plan as entirely fixed. Plans need to be flexible rather than rigid. Also, there have to be strong links between the school's vision and plans for improvement, plans need to be known by all involved, and they need to be constantly updated and modified in the light of changing circumstances and developments inside and outside the school. For this reason monitoring is vitally important to provide progress checks on how the plan is unfolding and being influenced by situational factors. Therefore, while having a plan is important, the process of planning is equally important and often on-going.

By 'monitoring' we mean the collection of information and evidence about a chosen topic under review. This topic could be a curriculum area, a child or group of children, an activity in the classroom (e.g. boys working together; pupils use of the book corner) or an aspect of a teacher's practice (e.g. questioning skills; classroom organization; use of praise). The purpose of monitoring is not to judge this information or evidence, simply to gather it in. Judgment comes later, which is why many today talk of monitoring and evaluation – the two are linked but separate activities.

Involvement

Improving schools seem to have ways of working that encourage staff, governors, parents and pupils to feel involved. These ways of working provide support for the school's efforts, as well as a range of additional resources that can often be used to enhance learning opportunities and other participants in the monitoring and reflection processes. At their strongest these feelings of involvement create a sense of community and commitment to high standards. Thus schools should have policies for encouraging the involvement of pupils, staff, parents, governors and other members of the school's community. Such participation has to be encouraged by procedures. For example, the organization of meetings should ensure that representatives from a cross-section of stakeholders are present. Minutes of meetings should be circulated to all. In these ways access to information is facilitated by the creation of an open climate. Similarly, the involvement of external support agencies has to be carefully planned. When staff from the LEA, or other consultants, are 'brought in' what do we want them to do, and how, and by when?

Staff Development

Schools will not improve unless teachers, individually and collectively, develop. Teachers' professional growth lies at the heart of school improvement. While teachers can often develop their professional practice on an individual basis, if the whole school is to develop then there need to be many opportunities for the staff to learn together – in key stage groups, year groups and as a whole staff. Such collaborative learning need not be something extra to do; it can occur as part of teachers working together. However, it is crucial that staff development activities are, in the main, focused on the classroom. Staff development programmes therefore need to be school based and classroom focused. There also needs to be a school policy for professional learning.

Coordination

Schools are busy places with many things happening at once. During the course of a week in school there will also be numerous events and incidents that are unplanned and unexpected. It is therefore important that those things we do want to happen are coordinated so that staff are kept informed and involved. When things are changing coordination is simply vital, otherwise staff will complain they do not know what is happening, when and why. Communication within the school is clearly an important aspect of coordination. In effect, the idea of coordination requires someone (or a pair of teachers) to act as project manager for the improvement priority that is being developed. These managers are the project coordinators and they have to develop the skills of working with colleagues, create the work groups, teams and manage their meetings so that they accomplish their agreed tasks, establish systems of communication and plan and monitor them, create and sustain dialogues about teaching and the improvement of practice.

Leadership

The way leadership is conceptualized and perceived within a school is a factor which influences the school's capacity to cope with change and undertake improvement work. Those schools addressing leadership as a major area for development, and which move from transactional to transformational leadership models (*see* Southworth, 1998), are usually maximizing capacity by establishing a clear vision for the school's development, valuing and using colleagues' task relevant experience and knowledge, working towards consensus without losing critical thinking and recognizing that leadership is a function to which many staff contribute, rather than being a set of responsibilities vested in a single person in a particular organizational position.

These six conditions are important to the school's chances of successfully achieving improvement priorities. However, two further points need to be made. First, these conditions interrelate. For example, leadership relates to coordination and planning, and involvement is a condition which relates to planning, coordination, enquiry and reflection and staff development, while staff development ranges across all of them. Second, the list is not an exhaustive one. These are six of the conditions, not *the* six conditions!

Since these six conditions were articulated we have become increasingly aware that all of them need to explicitly and frequently attend to not only the quality of pupils' *learning* (and sometimes the quality of staff professional learning), but also there needs to be a firm resolution and intent to focus on the quality of *teaching*. There is a clear case for focusing on teaching in primary schools, as we have argued elsewhere (Southworth, 1996), yet it remains one of the areas too many teachers and headteachers are reluctant to talk about. To 'improve teaching and disseminate good pedagogic practice, teachers must draw out and describe and, by implication, defend practice which has become second nature' (Millett, 1998).

Many schools have developed systems of monitoring, enquiry and reflection, but in our experience these generally favour the examination of pupils' learning achievements and progress and curricular provision. Monitoring of teaching is often the weakest area of monitoring, with many teachers reluctant to observe colleagues, to be observed themselves, or to comment on colleagues' teaching. Yet, if monitoring only looks at curricular provision and pupils' learning without considering what either or both mean for the teaching, then staff may be missing the very point of school-based enquiry, which is to strengthen the ways teachers and other staff meet children's learning needs.

Staff cannot escape from the requirement to develop their teaching. This requirement is vital not because the quality of teaching is necessarily poor, but because the challenge of teaching is great and because the demands on teachers are ever more extensive and complex (Southworth, 1996). Although attention to teaching is implied in the six conditions described above, there may now be a case for suggesting that it warrants a seventh condition on its own.

Certainly there is a good case for ensuring that enquiry and reflection encompasses a classroom focus that deals with both pupils' learning and teachers' pedagogy. Classroom enquiries need to look at the pupils' learning, the received curriculum (as well as the planned and the taught curricula) and use the data to ask questions about teaching. Enquiry needs to enable teachers to talk about their teaching, for them to observe and be observed teaching, for feedback sessions to be conducted and for teachers to prepare individual development plans that include attention to their teaching skills and competencies.

When enquiry creates an evidence-based approach to teaching and learning, then professional curiosity takes root and professional challenges and problems 'are treated as natural, expected phenomena and are looked for' (Fullan, 1993, p. 26). Such enquiry is *problem seeking* because teaching is often a puzzle and the puzzles that teachers' encounter are diverse in nature (e.g. how to ask higher order questions in certain subject areas, when to use group work, what pace to work at with mixed ability and mixed aged classes). Moreover, success in school change efforts

> Requires problem-finding techniques like 'worry lists', and regular review of problem-solving decisions at subsequent meetings to see what happened. Since circumstances and context are constantly changing, sometimes in surprising ways, an embedded spirit of constant enquiry is essential. Says Pascale (1990, p. 14) 'enquiry is the engine of vitality and self-renewal'. (Fullan, 1993, p. 26)

As Fullan (1993) goes on to argue, enquiry, action research, monitoring, reflection and evaluation develop norms, habits and techniques for continuous professional learning (p. 15). We wholeheartedly agree. In our experience, when teachers observe colleagues and are observed themselves, given that some ground-rules have been established, then the process is a powerful form of professional development for teachers and headteachers.

In turn, such processes play a major part in establishing 'learning enriched' schools (Rosenholtz, 1989). When 'problems are our friends' we can see numerous professional learning opportunities:

> Problems, then, are not just hassles to be dealt with and set aside. Lurking inside each problem is a workshop on the nature of organisations and a vehicle for personal growth. This entails a shift; we need to value the process of finding the solution – juggling the inconsistencies that meaningful solutions entail. (Pascale, 1990, p. 263)

Looked at this way, the improvement process is essentially a learning experience; change is learning (Fullan, 1993, p. 27).

This idea is presently taking hold in the thinking of many teachers. Some see schools as learning organizations (Holly and Southworth, 1989; Southworth, 1998a). Others refer to developing a 'culture of achievement' (Loose, 1997). According to Loose an achievement culture is an environment where:

- everyone in the school values learning and achievement
- teachers do not ask 'what is wrong with these pupils?' but rather 'what is wrong with the way we are tackling their problems and needs?'
- the school is communicating vibrantly that it has high standards and high expectations of its pupils and staff
- staff reflect about what they know about the pupils and harness this knowledge and awareness to drive the school forward. (Loose, 1997, p. 33)

When Loose goes on to describe two schools with such a culture, not only does she highlight the central role of enquiry, monitoring, reflection and evaluation, but also how these processes are educative and developmental for the staff. For these reasons it is worth citing Loose's description in full:

> The teachers set high standards for themselves and recognise the importance of sharing good practice. All ideas are welcomed and considered. At Robsack Wood Primary School, for example, it became clear that a newly qualified teacher had an effective way of assessing children's progress in science. When this was noted by senior staff, it was immediately considered for possible development.

At Roughwood Junior School, a young teacher was recognised to have skills in one particular area of the curriculum. Senior management demonstrated how they valued this by giving her room to develop her curriculum area to help create a model for developing others.

Both schools have structures in place for the dissemination of good practice. Regular, well recorded staff meetings, where ideas and information is filtered through the management levels, encourage staff to consider new methods and to recognise that good ideas will be looked at and individual strengths valued and applauded.

Given this commitment by senior management, the staff themselves have developed as active and interactive teachers with a wide variety of teaching and learning strategies and styles. These vary according to need and include spells of instructional exposition and challenging tasks . . . The teachers assess the pupils and the quality of teaching carefully and use the information gathered to determine how they will modify planned work to improve individual learning. This is underpinned by focusing upon a well planned whole school curriculum. . . .

These schools are conscious of the need for greater teacher expertise in curriculum matters and the ways in which pupils learn most effectively. They work towards developing this together, using reflective and experimental approaches, disseminated through staff groups where ideas are discussed and fed back. (p. 35)

This extract embodies many of the ideas raised in this chapter. It shows how the six conditions for school improvement, plus a commitment to focus on the quality of teaching, can be established and sustained in schools.

What these learning schools show is two other features as well. First, staff will be professionally learning their way forward, individually, in teams and as a whole staff group. Also, much, indeed, most of this professional learning takes place in the workplace. Teachers are learning about each other's craft knowledge, experience and expertise. They are sharing this expertise and learning with and from one another in ways which are collaborative, well managed and beneficial to them all and to the children. Work-based professional learning is a taken for granted feature of teaching in these schools.

Second, the emphasis on professional development is not something which has been 'bolted on' to work in these two schools; it has been 'built into' the systems, structures and processes the school as an organization utilizes. Work-based professional learning and classroom-focused enquiry and action research have become accepted and 'normal' practice because the schools' organizational cultures promote these values and norms. These schools do not trumpet this way of working; they just do it!

Summary

Self-evaluation – a cycle of review, planning and action – lies at the heart of self-managing improving schools. Therefore, an evidence-based approach to management and leadership is vital to the school's health, development and continued success.

Such an outlook has a long tradition in education, although today this has been reshaped by several recent initiatives such as school inspections, target-setting and benchmarking. As a consequence of these developments self-evaluation at the turn of the century is both wider in its frame of reference and deeper in terms of the detail of the audit and analysis. Process and outcome indicators both need to be used as part of school and classroom evaluation and both quantitative and qualitative measures should be adopted and applied.

While the collection of information and evidence is vitally important, monitoring is not a substitute for improvement effort and action. Analysis should stimulate action. When it does an evidence-based approach to school improvement can flourish and develop.

Improving schools need to identify their priorities, goals and targets. These are the focus for improvement and the content of the desired changes agreed by the staff, governors and others. At the same time, staff in improving schools need to attend to developing certain conditions that ensure the school has the internal capacity to manage change and improve. These conditions include: enquiry and reflection; collaborative planning; the involvement of staff, pupils, governors, parents and others; staff development; coordination; leadership; a consistent focus on the quality of teaching and the development of teachers' craft knowledge and pedagogic skills.

Classroom enquiry and reflection is essential. Attention to teaching and learning is critical not because the quality of teaching and learning is necessarily poor and in need of remediation, but because improvement is continuous professional learning. Pedagogic puzzles and problems are a natural part of teaching. Therefore, enquiry should be problem-seeking because, when it is so, enquiry becomes the engine that drives improvement.

Such an outlook on enquiry, evidence and the analysis of teaching and learning processes and outcomes underscores the idea of 'learning schools'. Learning schools are places where all participants value learning, are learning their way forward and pupils' learning goes hand-in-hand with teachers' and other colleagues' professional learning.

Another way of summarizing much of this chapter's argument is to use the school improvement cycle traced by Birmingham LEA (*see*

Figure 1.1 *Birmingham LEA's cycle of school improvement*

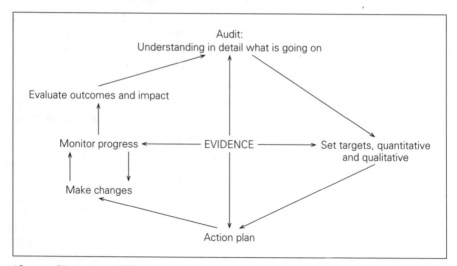

(*Source*: Birmingham LEA)

Figure 1.1). This is similar to the five-stage model of improvement used by the DfEE (1997). However, the Birmingham model is more interactive and puts evidence at the centre of the whole process.

When evidence is seen as at the centre of school improvement, and when all elements of the improvement process rely on evidence, then the case for an evidence-based approach to management and leadership becomes apparent. For this reason the ability to collect evidence and to use a range of techniques are important aspects of school improvement and of managers' and leaders' roles in improvement efforts.

Therefore, the next part of this book concentrates in detail on proven methods and techniques of gathering information for analysis, evaluation and action planning.

2   Collecting Evidence

If I reflect on some of my actions, analyse why I did what I did and what the consequences were for others, seek criticism from colleagues, read what others have done in similar circumstances, and test out my ideas by searching for evidence, I believe my judgement improves and so, in the heat of the moment when there is little time to think, I make better decisions. (Perry, 1978)

Introduction

As has been explained in the previous part, the major emphasis in this book is the importance of enquiry as a catalyst for improvements in the quality of teaching and learning. Walker (1985) has suggested that engaging in school-based enquiry is now seen as an essential element of the teacher's role

As teaching has become increasingly professionalised and the management of educational organisations more systematised, so 'enquiry' has become something that teachers are expected to include in their repertoire of skills. (p. 3)

Adopting a more systematic approach to the solution to problems encountered in the work context is progressively seen as the hallmark of those occupations that enjoy the label 'professional'. MacBeath et al. (1997, p. 9) argue that, as in many other professions, the commitment to critical and systematic reflection on practice as a basis for individual and collective development is at the heart of what it means to be a 'professional' teacher.

The increasing centralization of education practices could be seen as encouraging a view of teachers as 'mere implementers of government initiatives', whereas Carter and Halsall suggest that developing the skills of systematic enquiry leads teachers to become

Definers of their own reality through being able to investigate and reflect on self-chosen practices, and then modify these on the basis of

professional judgement, which engagement in the 'enquiry' process
has itself informed. (Carter and Halsall, 1998, pp. 71–72)

The introduction of the Education Reform Act in 1988 and succeeding
legislation has presented an unprecedented set of expectations to which
schools have been expected to respond. Whilst central government has
taken on more and more responsibility and control of the system, the
usual structures available to schools to support them in the processes of
implementation have been increasingly eroded and schools have had
to take on greater responsibility themselves for managing and coping
with the processes involved. Conner and Ainscow (1990, p. 1) recognize
this when they comment that the need for teachers to have effective
strategies for developing aspects of their practice is now more important than it has been in the past. Processes of collaborative enquiry and
development can be a powerful way of helping teachers and schools to
respond to and cope with many mandated requirements.

The importance of the development of the skills of enquiry are
also recognized by Hopkins (1993) who suggests that improvements in
teaching and learning are dependent on the qualities and skills of the
teacher

> It is becoming increasingly obvious that 'top-down' change does not
> 'mandate what matters', and that it is local implementation, the work
> of teachers, that determines student outcomes. (p. xii)

The advice of Stenhouse (1975) is at the heart of such claims. He
advocated the development of 'teachers as researchers', claiming that
there is 'no curriculum development without teacher development'.
This idea was revisited by Hargreaves (1992) who agreed with Stenhouse
that there is little likelihood of school development without teacher
development, but also argued that the obverse is true and that teacher
development is unlikely to take place without school development.
The thesis, therefore, is that engaging in enquiry is fundamental to
improving schools and that in the process it extends the professional
competence of the teachers involved. As Dudley (1999) has suggested,
perhaps it is time we thought of schools as research-based institutions
rather than teachers as researchers.

There is also evidence to suggest that gathering and using evidence about practices in school effectively contributes to improving outcomes for teachers and for students (Berwick, 1994). In Berwick's study,
which focused on improving the achievements of students in his school,
the development of the skills of enquiry led to increased knowledge

and confidence for the teachers and direct improvements in the achievements of many of the children.

Engaging in the processes of 'systematic enquiry' does not necessarily mean a detailed knowledge of the research or literature related to a particular area, however, or to high levels of proficiency in the skills associated with educational research. Instead it is more concerned with what is needed to cope with immediate issues in one's own institution, how to gather the appropriate evidence upon which to achieve an **informed** rather than an **intuitive** judgment. Langeveld (1965) reminds us that investigations into management issues facing a school or a specific classroom concern in need of solution are essentially practical

> in the sense that we do not only want to know facts and to understand relations for the sake of knowledge. We want to know and understand in order to be able to act and act 'better' than we did before. (cited in Conner and Ainscow, 1990, p. 1)

School and classroom enquiries are likely, therefore, to be associated with a range of different purposes. On the one hand, the pressure for such initiatives can be a direct result of an external stimulus; for example, the result of a demand from an LEA or central government. On the other hand it can result from an internal concern. It may be that an issue identified in the school development plan, which has been the focus of attention by the whole school for a term, now needs to be evaluated. Have the intentions and expectations been achieved? An enquiry of this kind is essential to see whether the investment of energy as well as any financial support has been justified. Alternatively, it may be necessary to find out what is currently happening before introducing something new, recognizing that what is actually happening need not necessarily be what is thought to be occurring. It is also the case that an interim investigation can provide useful information to steer an initiative to a more successful conclusion by supporting or redirecting the progress and processes of something newly introduced. Lewis and Munn (1987) reinforce the arguments presented so far when they suggest that the overall aim of these kind of investigations is

> to provide some systematic and reliable information that can be used as a basis for action. Instead of relying upon intuition and value judgements in making decisions, the individual teacher, the department or the school staff as a whole can use carefully collected evidence to feed into the decision making process. (pp. 6–7)

In the past, investigations of this kind have tended to have been undertaken by individual teachers, often as part of an award bearing in-service education course. We would argue that it is increasingly important that such studies be seen as collaborative exercises involving groups of teachers. The benefits of collaborative investigation are manifold as an increasing range of writers testify (Lewis and Munn, 1987; Hopkins, 1993; Bell, 1987; Halsall et al., 1998). The main advantages of working together on an issue include the fact that colleagues can support each other through the highs and lows of the process and sustain motivation and interest. They can bring together different perspectives and points of view, ensuring that any exploration is thorough and covers the full range of the issues involved as well as all perspectives represented by the staff group. It is also the case that the results of an investigation by a group, representing the staff, is more likely to have an effect on the thinking and practice of the whole staff and achieve more success-ful implementation. For example, the evidence from the IQEA project described in Part 1 supports this claim.

Hargreaves (1992) has argued that legislation in the early 1990s had a positive effect with the development of what he has described as a 'new professionalism', which entailed an increasing move within schools from **individualism** to **collaboration**. There is evidence to support this claim in studies of the implementation of the National Curriculum in primary schools (Pollard et al., 1994 and Osborn et al., 1997). Hargreaves also argues that changes in teacher education are influencing changes in professional practice in many schools from one of **supervision** to **mentoring**. This change

> presupposes a more explicit professional and reflective role on the part of the individual mentor-teacher, and an inevitable shift in social relations through the developing of new professional partnerships in schools. (Hopkins, 1993, p. 218)

A third feature of Hargreaves's 'new professionalism' is a move from **hierarchies** to **teams** amongst groups of teachers, which has become especially apparent in planning for the National Curriculum in primary schools and a reduction of idiosyncratic approaches which typified the practice of some primary teachers (Pollard et al., 1994, Osborn et al., 1997).

Despite this emphasis on the benefits of working with others, we would not want to deny the value of individual investigations in one's own classroom. Our concern, however, is for more consistency in the use of evidence for decision making and that the evidence that is used should have been collected systematically and within a set of clearly established and agreed principles. The range of possibilities is extensive. For example:

- An individual teacher may have identified a problem, an interest, or a concern within his or her own classroom and wishes to find out more to resolve a dilemma. This may be related to an individual child, a group of children, an aspect of the curriculum or a feature of the teacher's classroom management.
- A curriculum coordinator may need to explore the effectiveness of an aspect of the curriculum across the school with a view to changing policy, ensuring progression and continuity, or to focus the purchase of resources to support areas of strength or weakness.
- A group of teachers may wish to review a range of alternative curriculum proposals to judge their likely effect in practice before a whole school decision is made.
- As a result of the analysis of assessment results in the school, a number of issues might be identified, for which each teacher will gather information to report back to a later whole staff meeting, before decisions are made.
- The whole staff may need to evaluate practice, performance and policy in an area of teaching or administration.
- With the introduction of Local and National Targets for Literacy and Numeracy, there is a need to explore current achievements in order to set targets that are realistic and achievable for the school, as well as for individual classes and children.
- There may be a need to provide evidence and analysis of the school's programme for management purposes or to inform the LEA, Ofsted, school governors, parents or other interested parties. In such situations, clear and accessible evidence-based information is essential.
- There is also likely to be a need to interpret and assess information coming into schools from a variety of sources. For example, from central government, government agencies, examination boards, LEAs, test agencies, HMI, TTA, QCA or from research findings.
- Also there is a need to make effective use of information provided by agencies that are concerned with pupils but who do not necessarily share educational assumptions or use the language of schools: e.g. the social services, local community, local employers, etc.

As the above list suggests, the range of possibilities is endless. In order to use time effectively, we suggest there are a series of stages that aid the process, and they revolve around asking a series of fundamental questions about the proposed inquiry:

- What do we want to know? (and why?)
- How are we going to find out?
- What does this tell us?
- What are we going to do about it?

The following sections are organized in relation to the first two of these questions and the case studies in Part 3 provide illustrations of responses to the last two questions.

What Do We Want to Know? (and Why?)

Paying careful attention to this first question is essential. If it is appropriately addressed, it can save time and a great deal of later confusion and anxiety. The aim at this stage is to clarify the focus and to ensure that all involved are clear about the purpose of an enquiry. As we have suggested above, there is mounting evidence to suggest that school improvement can only occur when teachers are active partners in determining priorities for development in a school and generating strategies and policies for the implementation of any proposed changes in practice (Fullan, 1991).

It is essential, therefore, that a clear focus is identified and that whatever is identified is manageable, specific and achievable and that there are not too many initiatives under way at the same time. Hopkins (1985) offers some sensible advice

- Do not tackle something that you are unable to do anything about, that is unlikely to lead to any positive changes.
- Initially, make sure that the focus is small scale, with the intention being to achieve some success and a positive outcome.
- Choose a topic for inquiry that is of importance to the school and recognised as such. It is also important that the topic is of interest and therefore motivating to those to be involved. Tasks, wherever possible, should be seen as a part of normal activity and not a burden. (p. 47)

Kemmis and McTaggart (1988) have also written on the theme of 'issue identification' and suggest that you do not have to begin with a 'problem'. All you need is a general idea that something might be improved. Your general idea may stem from a promising new idea or the recognition that current practice falls short of aspiration. Another example of this process can be seen in the work of MacBeath, Boyd et al. (1997), who argue that there are three fundamental questions that need to be asked of enquiries of the kind being discussed.

- What particular aspects of the school would benefit from investigation for improvement?
- Why is this needed at this time?
- Who needs this information? Teachers, school managers, governors, pupils, parents, the local Authority, central government? (p. 10)

Simpson and Tuson (1995) suggest that by thinking through and writing down exactly what information you want to collect and what you think it will demonstrate, you begin to make explicit your underlying assumptions. As a result, assumptions can be examined and challenged and alternative viewpoints considered. In engaging in such a process it enables the enquirer(s) to determine the nature, scope, involvement, evidence sources and processes to be adopted.

In today's schools, however, starting with such an open agenda is likely to be seen as a luxury. With so many initiatives requiring careful scrutiny and consideration, it is probably much more sensible to focus attention on initiatives identified in the school development plan or action plan, or on issues that are likely to be part of the plan in the near future. An enquiry of the latter kind can lay the groundwork for future development.

As suggested earlier, we have found that an effective way into clarifying the focus of investigations is to use questions. For example:

Questions that Can Start an Enquiry

- What is actually happening now in . . . ?
- What ought to be happening now in . . . ?
- What can I/we do about . . . ?
- Do I/we need to improve . . . ?
- Are some of us unhappy about . . . ?
- I have an idea that we ought to . . .

These can be answered individually or collectively. The analysis of the answers helps to clarify the focus. The procedure of starting from questions derived from school or classroom issues has a long history and is the basis of a very well established Open University Course that engages teachers and others in investigations in their own work contexts. The course 'The Curriculum in Action' (Ashton et al., 1981) invites responses from participants to six 'deceptively simple' questions, three of which focus upon the teacher and three on the learners.

1   What were the learners actually doing?
2   What were they learning?
3   How worthwhile was it?
4   What did you/we do?
5   What did you/we learn?
6   What will you/we do next?

Answers to each of these questions demand systematic enquiry and teachers who have participated in the course soon realize that to gather evidence related to each of them can be very eye-opening, especially if in answer to the second question it soon appears that they are not learning anything! As Drummond, Shreeve et al. (1994) suggest:

> Don't be misled by the everyday language of the questions into thinking that the answers are quick and simple. They are not easy to answer. Indeed, the longer you think about them, the more complicated they can become. Each question and the explorations you need to make to answer it leads to other questions and further explanation. (p. 8)

There are also a whole range of school review strategies that might also be drawn upon to extend the ideas offered here. One of the classic examples of this is the GRIDS programme (Guidelines for the Review and Internal Development of Schools), which was a former Schools Council project based at the University of Bristol (McMahon et al., 1984). Despite the fact that this material was developed before the National Curriculum, the processes that were developed by the project are still useful. The materials from the GRIDS project were aimed at helping teachers to review and develop the curriculum and organization of their school. An anonymously completed questionnaire is used to allow all staff to express their views about the school's strengths and weaknesses and to identify aspects of the school which should be the focus of a specific review. This is then tackled by a 'specific review team' who collect, analyse and make recommendations in the light of the analysis for discussion and consideration by the whole staff. More recently, the National Union of Teachers has sponsored the development of a similar framework for school self-evaluation (MacBeath, Boyd et al., 1997) in which they argue that

> Whilst evaluation has different purposes and is founded on different values, it is generally agreed that evaluation involves gathering information to help decision-making. In a school context, therefore, any information or insight which assists the process of decision-making may be regarded as a form of evaluation. The key practical task is to decide what information may be required and how it might be gathered. (p. 9)

School self-evaluation has been advocated in a recent report from Ofsted (1998), which emphasizes that the most important focus should be the effectiveness of teaching and learning in a school. The report distinguishes between seven different approaches that are currently used in schools and considers their relative strengths with regard to focusing on teaching and learning. The **checklist** approach evaluates practice against a list of questions, often generated by the school. The report suggests that such questions rarely focus on the quality of teaching and learning, nor do they promote the collection of solid evidence about the quality and standards of work in a school. The **ballot** approach is typified by GRIDS, which Ofsted suggests tends to focus on curriculum planning systems and policies rather than the quality of classroom work. The **curriculum-led** approach is a pragmatic approach, most often used in primary schools, where one or two areas of the curriculum are identified for review each year. 'Review' normally appears to mean drawing up yet another 'new scheme of work'. The weakness is that such reviews tend to focus on coverage and design of the curriculum rather than its effectiveness in developing knowledge, understanding and skills, with a focus on raising standards. The fourth approach is described as the **appraisal** approach, related to school appraisal schemes, which are admitted as not having been particularly effective in improving the quality of teaching and learning in many schools. The **child-centred** approach involves the school in surveying the views and attitudes of pupils, parents and other interested parties. They suggest that relatively few schools ask pupils for their views about the quality of the teaching in their school (although our experience of schools which use this approach is very positive). The **quality mark** approach has been adopted by some schools, who seek external recognition of their work through, for example, School Curriculum Awards. Occasion-ally this may pay attention to aspects of teaching and learning, but it tends to consider finished products. The final version is described as **school self-evaluation**, which to be effective should objectively review pupils' achievements and identify areas of under-achievement, account for results by identifying strengths and weaknesses in the quality and effectiveness of practices in the school and develop a school improve-ment plan which identifies areas for improvement and establishes the means by which evidence will be gathered related to these areas.

In an attempt to organize thinking at the early stage of an enquiry there are a number of important factors to take into consideration (of course it is recognized that they may not all be appropriate).

- First attempt to produce a clear outline of the issue to be invest-igated, with some justification for its consideration against other competing priorities. Why this issue rather than something else?
- Then consider the main purposes that such an enquiry will satisfy.
- You will then need to reflect upon the possible influences on the enquiry: where, when, who with, over what timescale and with what product in mind?
- Having clarified the above issues, you may then need to con-sider other useful sources of advice. Is there any research or literature that might extend your understanding? Are there other schools in the locality that have addressed similar concerns? Can the local adviser be of any help? Have you any contacts with Higher Education that might extend your understanding and help you to develop and produce a manageable and secure framework?
- If the enquiry requires classroom visits and observations, when will these take place and who by? What implications will this have for the plan and for the investigation?
- Are there any school documents that will be needed and are these easily accessible?

All of these help to refine the investigation and the identification of relevant questions that should make the process more manageable by clearing away potential difficulties before data collection starts. The process of refinement is often best undertaken as a group. Participation in the process prepares people for later participation, even if only as a source of information. Given that investigations of the kind we are discussing are likely to involve a whole range of other people, their behaviour and their points of view, it is important to spend some time considering the ethical implications of the information that is to be gathered, especially how it is collected and how it is going to be used. Elliott (1991) suggests that the most important issues that must be addressed are **confidentiality, negotiation** and **control**. He argues that confidential information should be treated as such and not released more widely without the agreement of those who provided the information. Similarly, even though a project might have been agreed it is still important to negotiate with specific individuals who might provide information for the investigation and in fulfilling both of these criteria it ensures that participants feel they have some control over the process. As Bassey (1995) suggests:

> in taking and using data from persons, [we] should do so in ways which recognise those persons' initial ownership of the data and which respect them as fellow human beings who are entitled to dignity and privacy. (p. 15)

A variety of publications offer further advice concerning the ethical basis of school-based investigation (see, for example, Hopkins, 1993; Bell, 1987; Walker, 1985; Kemmis and McTaggart, 1988; Elliott, 1991; Simons, 1987).

Having clarified the focus of an inquiry and established a framework and timeline for its enactment, the next stage is to consider the most appropriate ways of gathering all the necessary information. The next section introduces the most effective ways of gathering evidence, and will focus particularly on the processes of collecting data through:

1   classroom observation
2   interviews
3   questionnaires
4   documentary analysis
5   the analysis of assessment information

How Are We Going to Find Out?

1. Observation

The process of observation has progressively increased in importance as a central source of information for the development of schools, the improvement of classroom practice and standards of children's achievement, a view that is endorsed in a variety of studies. For example, Hopkins (1993) argues:

> Observation plays a crucial role, not only in classroom research, but also more generally in supporting the professional growth of teachers and in the process of school development . . . it seems to be the pivotal activity that links together reflection for the individual teacher and collaborative enquiry for pairs or groups of teachers. It also encourages the development of a language for talking about teaching and provides a means for working on developmental priorities for the staff as a whole. (p. 76)

Also, Foster (1996) recognizes the importance of observation as a fundamental means of data collection in a wide variety of contexts and for an increasing range of purposes when he says

> In recent years, what goes on in schools has come under increasing scrutiny. The behaviour of teachers, students and others in classrooms, staffrooms, corridors and playgrounds has been researched more frequently and more closely than ever before. Academics have conducted research in order to describe and explain the social processes occurring in schools and thereby gain a better understanding of the complexity of our education system. Equally, under the influence of the teacher-as-researcher movement, an increasing number of teachers have begun to research their own schools and classrooms more systematically. Recently, more teachers have begun to research their colleague's practice for the purpose of training, appraisal and review, while inspectors are more regularly researching school practice in order to evaluate the quality of current provision. The main technique used . . . is **observation**. (back page)

Drummond, Rouse et al. (1992) describe observation as an essential and invaluable part of any educator's skills:

> Observation means more than watching and listening; it is a process by which educators can understand and give meaning to what they see and hear, drawing on their own knowledge and experience, as well as the evidence of their senses. Observation means more than ticking off items on a checklist to establish efficiency or productivity; it enables educators to give a full and useful account of children's learning and development. Observation means more than rating children's development on a numerical scale; observation reveals the richness and complexity of children's learning.
> Observing children plays a crucial part in developing and monitoring a quality curriculum for all children. (p. 42)

The Why, What and How of Observation, or, Going Beyond Looking to Seeing

> Lasting change in education comes not from central advisers and re-searchers handing down pre-packaged innovations, but from individual pioneers modifying their practice in response to **observation** of their own pupils. (Griffin-Beale, 1984)

This comment from Christian Schiller says it all: observation of and reflection upon events and activities that go on in the classroom is a fundamental feature of effective classrooms, as the above comments testify. Skill in observation is one of the most important skills that the teacher possesses and it is one that should be continually worked on to improve our understanding of children and their learning. It is important to remember that reflecting upon and refining one's observational skills focuses upon abilities that are a natural human resource. Observation is central to our understanding of the world around us, but as a result we can often undertake our observations intuitively and rely on our first impressions our 'gut response', when further reflection might lead us to alternative interpretations. Joan Dean (1993) elaborated on this when she said:

> Normal living involves us all in the process of making judgements about people and events in order to predict what may happen and decide what to do next. We do this from a very early age and it becomes our normal response to new situations. This is evident when you go to a course or if you are on holiday and meet new people. You listen to them, look at them and ask questions to discover the ways in which they are like you and the ways in which they differ and what their interests are and so on. The judgements you make may not always be accurate, but this may not matter in such circumstances, particularly if you are aware that you are making judgements on inadequate evidence. As a professional teacher, however, you need to be much more sure of your evidence because much depends upon the outcome of your judgements. You therefore need to extend the everyday practice of making judgements (based upon your observations) in order to make sure that the judgements you make are as valid as possible. (p. 25)

Such concerns are even more important in the current educational context where assessment seems to dominate everything that we do. Developing observational skills can contribute to our assessments but they can also extend our understanding of what is going on in our classrooms.

Conner (1991) has commented that not only do we learn more about children and their learning by improved observation, we also learn more about the learning process and our involvement in it.

So, having made a passionate defence of and justification for the place of observation, what do we really mean by observation, and more importantly, how can you do it given all the other demands on time in the primary school?

What Is Observation?

One of the ways in which our understanding of classroom observation was extended was through the work of Harlen. In her project on progress in learning science (published under the title *Match and Mismatch* in 1978), which focused on ways in which an individual teacher might use observation in her own classroom, she posed the question, How can we really monitor children's progress? The solution the project team developed was to use observations of children in action, but for the purposes of their investigation they saw observation as being more than just looking. It involved:

- **Looking** at the way children go about their work and not just what they produce. In other words, the processes employed by children are an important source of information, which means that it is acceptable for us to watch children at work and not feel that we have constantly to be 'teaching'.
- **Listening** to pupils' ideas and trying to gain an understanding of their reasoning. This means that teachers need to learn to stand back and try not to intervene. It is often the case that if children are left alone, they move towards a successful solution on their own.
- **Discussing** problems, responses and interpretations with children so that they reveal their ways of thinking to us. This implies that we have to create the space for this to happen.

Clearly each of these proposals have important implications for classroom management, particularly if the observation is being undertaken by a teacher in his or her own classroom. If you believe in the value and potential of classroom observation, a particular kind of classroom is needed. This has recently been debated in a project that focused on observation in the early years (Stierer et al., 1993), where the following comments were made:

Observation-led teaching requires careful planning if it is to become something routine and automatic rather than something done during the odd moment when an opportunity presents itself. This will suggest a classroom organised around activities which do not require constant teacher supervision, direction and involvement. Examples of such activities are group problem solving tasks which require children to work and talk collaboratively. (p. 9)

And:

In order to feel free to observe children and to be able to write notes in the middle of a busy classroom, it is essential that the children are as independent as possible. You will need to ensure that they are not coming to you with problems they could sort out for themselves . . . so that the time is spent in quality interaction and evaluation of what is going on, rather than in low level maintenance. (p. 24)

They go on to list the following questions, many of which are obvious, to support observation in the classroom and to help the development of children's independence.

- Are resources readily available and accessible to the children?
- Do they know how to use resources efficiently and effectively?
- Do they know where to put finished products?
- Do activities and provision stimulate prolonged involvement?
- What activities are you creating to develop and encourage self reliance?

A further series of questions are asked to help development here. For example:

- Do they know what to do if they are stuck and are unable to turn to you?
- Do they ask each other for help or volunteer to help others?
- Do they try alternative strategies?

That's all very well, we hear you say, but you don't know what my class is like! In such situations, our advice is to involve the children themselves, simply by explaining that you wish to look at what is going on in the classroom in order to make things better and that the only way you can do this is to spend some time looking at what is happening without them disturbing you. Sometimes a signal is needed, by, for example, suggesting that carrying a 'red folder' is an indication that you are observing and are not to be disturbed. (We have worked with teachers who have used a wide variety of such signals, from 'My Roger Red Hat' to 'My Invisible Badge'.)

One teacher who tried this commented:

> I was amazed, I expected them to need my attention. I did as you suggested and said to my class (of 5-year-olds) if they needed help while I was observing they could either ask someone on their table, or wait for me to put my folder down. I started with a couple of minutes on one child and now I am able to concentrate for quite long periods. The fascinating thing is that I've begun to see things I never noticed before.

Another teacher of older juniors commented:

> The children responded magnificently because they really felt they were helping me and my first session was spent in writing down whatever came to mind . . . I found that the children needed to be settled in activities that they were able to work at reasonably independently. Now the children are used to my activities they respond extremely well, enabling me to carry out some very worthwhile observations within my classroom (now without the folder!).

A group of teachers who have employed this technique offer the following advice:

- Prepare for your observation: consider all possible interruptions and attempt to divert them before they happen.
- Prepare your focus: one child, a group of children, a particular activity.
- If the focus is to be one child, develop strategies to reduce anxiety or ensure that s/he remains unaware that they are the focus of attention.
- Prepare beforehand any relevant notes, questions or observation schedules.

Having made some suggestions as to how an individual teacher might create the space for classroom observation on his/her own, the next important question relates to what one actually does? In response to this question, we would argue that observation should certainly be **purposeful**. In other words, as we have suggested earlier, what you do depends on what you want to find out. Once you are clear about the purpose, the procedure to adopt to satisfy that purpose becomes much easier. It is important at the start, however, not to try to do too much or to observe for too long.

Hook (1985) offers some useful advice:

> Classroom observation is more than just sitting and watching. It is looking with a purpose, using techniques to record or encode what is observed. The ability to observe is not innate or inherited. It is developed systematically and progressively from simple beginnings, with the observation of one child, a specific behaviour, or a simple scene, to more elaborate settings with complex means of identifying and recording . . . behaviour. (p. 17)

Observational Strategies

The comment above by Hook takes us on to the range of observational strategies that are available to us. Figure 2.1 illustrates the range in the form of two continuums:

Figure 2.1   Modes of observation

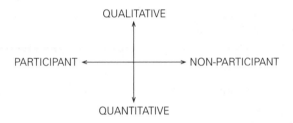

These offer a distinction between those techniques that are more **qualitative** (i.e. we note down behaviours and reactions in written form – a narrative account of what is observed) and those techniques that are more **quantitative**, where we would record the number of times something happens. Quantitative procedures use tick lists and sets of criteria that structure observations and they often produce percentages of time spent on a particular activity.

A second dimension of observation distinguishes the extent of the observer's involvement. A **participant** observer stays close to the action and when there is misunderstanding or the need for further clarification would be likely to ask questions of the children (i.e. look, listen and discuss). This form of observation can be undertaken by the teacher or by another observer. A **non-participant** observer tends to stay apart from the action and records on the basis of his or her interpretation of events, often using predetermined schedules. Such procedures tend to be employed more often in large-scale projects, but many teachers have developed their own observational schedules based on their knowledge

tion. It is also the procedure that is much more likely to be
:n observing other teachers, as a manager, or to collect data
‿‿‿‿ool-focused investigation. The following example illustrates an
observational schedule developed by a group of teachers for gathering
information on children's behaviour in group work situations. Using
these categories the teachers attempted to monitor the children's participation in a focused way.

To what extent is 'X' able to

offer ideas and take initiative? ....
modify views in the light of the views of others? ....
take on a different role as required by the group? ....
take an appropriate share of the task? ....
persevere with the task? ....
offer a range of alternative solutions? ....
show sensitivity to the needs and limitations of others in the
    group? ....
share the resources available and manage them effectively? ....

What emerged from this experience were difficulties over when and
how often observations were needed to be able to provide a reasonably accurate reflection of the children's involvement. A number of
possible strategies exist.

Time Sampling Here the observer notes down the particular
behaviour at regular moments for a specified period. For example,
every 2 minutes for a period of 10 minutes, or in the case of the group
work schedule illustrated above, each child was observed for 5 minutes
with a note of the specific behaviour at 30-second intervals. This provides the observer with a sample of behaviour related to the categories
provided.

Frequency Sampling An alternative to time sampling is to select
a particular aspect of behaviour and note every time it occurs over a set
period of time. This procedure gives a reasonably accurate measure of
the frequency of certain behaviours. If it is used regularly, it can help to
find out if something is increasing or decreasing. It can be used to
monitor progress, or something that is causing difficulties; it can also be
used with individuals and with groups of children.

Duration Sampling This technique allows exploration of how
much time is spent on a particular activity by an individual or a group
of children. So, for example, a teacher might focus on one child and

note down every time a particular behaviour is observed, when and where it took place and how long it went on for.

Question Framing A less structured approach to organizing observations in classrooms is to frame a series of questions that can be used as a guide to the information that needs to be collected. For example, the *Primary Language Record* (Barrs et al., 1988) suggests that observation of a child reading silently will reveal ways in which s/he approaches the task, and that it is possible to identify the strategies being used. When the child reads aloud, other strategies may be revealed. They suggest that during observations of reading the observer needs to notice:

- whether the child uses illustrations (initially to help retell the story, later to check guesses)
- whether the child makes use of the context to help work out the meaning; does what s/he read makes sense
- whether the child reads in meaningful 'chunks', or word by word
- whether the child uses the structure of language to help work out the meaning
- whether the child uses knowledge about books and written language to help work out meaning
- whether the child uses knowledge of what words/letters look or sound like to help work out unknown words
- whether s/he makes a good guess at unknown words or waits to be told
- whether s/he is using several strategies to get meaning from the text or has a heavy dependence on one strategy (e.g. phonic analysis)
- whether the child self-corrects, and seems to be monitoring her/his own reading (p. 28)

The implication of this example is to reinforce the comments of Hook cited earlier. Observations need preparation.

One of the difficulties many teachers experience when adopting qualitative procedures for classroom observations is the problem of what to note down, and how and where to note it so that it is manageable. To some extent this depends on personal preference. Some observers need to be systematic and focused for a specific period of time each week with two or three children as the targets; as a result, over a relatively short time every child becomes a focus for attention. Other observers keep a notebook and during these occasions record on the spot whatever appears to be significant. The notes become sources for conversations with the observer to be used in future planning and as a source of information when compiling comments on children's progress or a teacher's behaviour or actions. Other teachers are unhappy with this and like to make notes as and when something significant occurs. The problem with this is that some children can easily be missed and important information easily forgotten or misrepresented. Note-taking for some is something that is done after the event, or rough notes are kept for later modification. We have seen some teachers using 'Post-its' for this purpose, where these are put together in a more coherent form later that day. However it is done, some form of system is needed that gathers this information together and the development of quick note-taking skills are necessary. Over time we have found that we have developed a series of shorthand procedures: for example, using arrows to indicate movement and single letters to indicate particular children, or hieroglyphics to indicate behaviours, as can be seen in Table 2.1.

Whatever procedures you adopt, it is important that the information you have generated is of use to you. If it isn't, change the procedure. It is also important to engage in a process of reflection on what the information is telling you. This is often best done with other teachers who can bring a fresh set of professional eyes to your interpretations and extend your understanding.

Hopkins (1993) distinguishes between four methods of classroom observation: **open, focused, structured** and **systematic**. In an **open** observation, it is exactly that: the observer simply notes down what strikes him or her as being of importance. It is basically noting down the key issues, ideas or concerns that were drawn to the observer's attention. The record of events can then serve as the basis of discussion between observer and teacher after the observation. One of the weaknesses of this approach is that the information generated serves no particular purpose. Table 2.2 provides a typical structure for such observations.

An alternative to this very open approach is to use some previously agreed headings to provide a limited structure to the observations. This acts as a filter to the observation and offers a focus for the observer. These more **focused** observations are based upon previously agreed aspects of practice, as was illustrated by the categories described earlier for working in groups. Other examples might include a teacher who wishes to collect some information on the effectiveness of her grouping strategies, or her questioning techniques, or the ways in which she works with the boys in her classroom. The aim of the observation is to record behaviours of both the teacher and the children in relation to

Table 2.1 An illustration of narrative recording

CHILD'S INITIALS: A.N. SEX: boy AGE: 4/11 DATE AND TIME OBSERVED: 18/11 10.50			
ACTIVITY RECORD	LANGUAGE RECORD	TASK	SOCIAL
1 TC at woodwork table, hammers nail into wood. Goes round table & looks at small metal pieces. Offers nail to A.	TC → A: Will you bang this? A → TC (bangs nail in)	SSC	PAIR
2 Watches A carefully. Gives A a bottle cap to hammer on for him	A → TC (about hammering) TC → A (asks her to hammer on cap)	SSC	PAIR
3 Watches A hammering his bottle cap & milk bottle top into wood with nail. A finishes – hands TC his wood. (looms like →)		SSC	PAIR
4 Carries woodwork outside, back indoors. Takes it to paint. Paints it blue, with brush		ART	SOL
5 Paints his woodwork. Paints, wipes thumb on paper, on wood.		ART	SOL
6 Paints his woodwork.		ART	SOL
7 Takes coat off – gets apron and puts it on. Continues to paint	A → TC: Not with your coat on, you'll get it all over	ART	SOL
8 Paints woodwork	A → TC: Now finish that and come and have your milk. TC → A: No! A → TC: We'd save some then	ART	PAIR
9 Looks at hands – goes to washbowl in corner (leaves woodwork on paint table). Washes with 1 C	TC ↔ C TC ↔ C A → TC + C (about washing)	DA	PAIR
10 Washes hands, dries them. Goes to sit at milk table, next to twin brother. Helper gives him cap	TC → A: Where's mine? I haven't got a cup. TC → C: I got a blue one	DA	LG

Note: SSC: small scale construction. ART: free expression art activity. SOL: solitary.
DA: domestic activity. (PAIR) means the child is chatting with a helper. (LG): in a large group of more than six children.
(*Source:* Sylva et al., 1980)

39

Table 2.2 An 'open observation' recording format

Date:	Time:	Place:
Observation:		

Time	Observation Notes

that issue and nothing else. Again, the resulting information can be used for discussion with a view to improvement. In focused observations, school issues can also be addressed. In a study undertaken for a primary school, one aspect of their practice had been criticized during an Ofsted inspection. The members of staff felt that this had been misrepresented, so they invited an outside observer, who was also a trained Ofsted inspector, to undertake a series of focused observations related to this issue as part of their *post*-Ofsted action plan. A report on the findings was sent to Ofsted and also used to modify and change their practice. The focus had arisen from an external stimulus. There was agreement amongst the staff that it was an issue that should be addressed and agreement that it was best undertaken by an external observer, in whom they had trust. On that basis, they were prepared to act on the findings.

Structured observations usually employ systems to record activities in some kind of quantitative form. In the example described earlier, related to problem solving, some of the teachers tallied the number of times individuals fulfilled particular criteria, while others wrote a narrative. With a tally system, the observer simply ticks every time a particular activity occurs. For example, the fact that 'David took the lead and showed initiative', could have been recorded in the following ways:

	9.05	9.17	9.20	9.23
offer ideas and take initiative....	✓	✓	✓	✓

offer ideas and take initiative.... 9.05   David suggested a good idea which was used by the group.
9.17   David followed up F's ideas to good effect.

Figure 2.2 Observation using a diagram for recording (i)

Date: Time: Place:

Observation of:

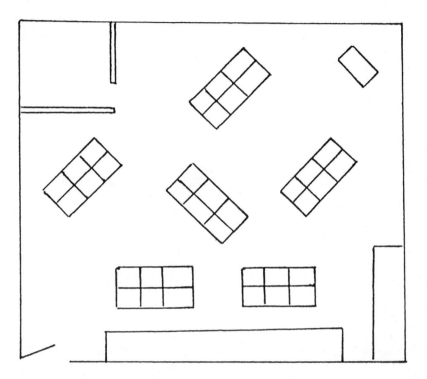

Focus: Pupil Involvement
Draw a diagram of the classroom and indicate where each pupil is sitting.
Each time a pupil gets involved in the lesson in any of the following ways, write the code
number against the pupil.
1   Answers a question voluntarily.
2   Answers a question when asked.
3   Volunteers a comment or view.
4   Makes a disruptive comment.

An alternative to a tally system is to use diagrams as the basis of
the data collection from observations. Figures 2.2 and 2.3 illustrate the
ways in which this procedure can be used. (These examples came from
a classroom observation resource pack produced by our colleague
Michael Fielding.) The first example requires a diagram of the classroom layout.

The second illustration of using diagrams for recording observations comes from Bellon et al. (1982), which demonstrates a means of
recording children's responses in large group discussions (Figure 2.3).

Figure 2.3 Observation using a diagram for recording (ii): Record of student responses in large group discussion

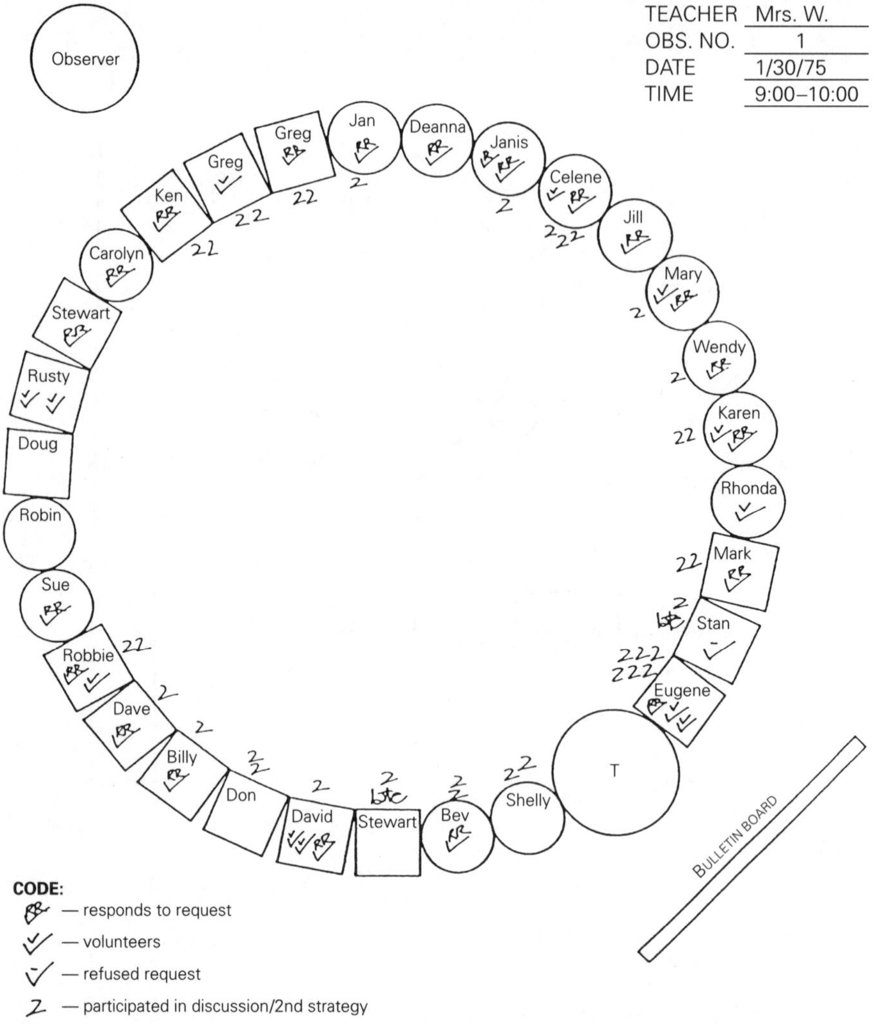

TEACHER Mrs. W.
OBS. NO. 1
DATE 1/30/75
TIME 9:00–10:00

CODE:
ℛℰ — responds to request
✓✓ — volunteers
✓̌ — refused request
2 — participated in discussion/2nd strategy

(*Source:* J. J. Bellon et al. (1982) *Classroom Supervision and Instructional Improvement: A Synergetic Process*, Kendall/Hunt Publishing Company, Dubuque, IA.)

Figure 2.4 illustrates observation of the involvement of children during a reading lesson and notes their behaviour every three minutes according to a set of previously determined criteria; whether they were on task, independently reading (A); on task and reading with the teacher (B); out of their seat (C); talking with a friend (D); out of the room (E); or playing (F). This example was adapted from Acheson and Gall (1980).

Figure 2.4   Observation using a diagram for recording (iii)

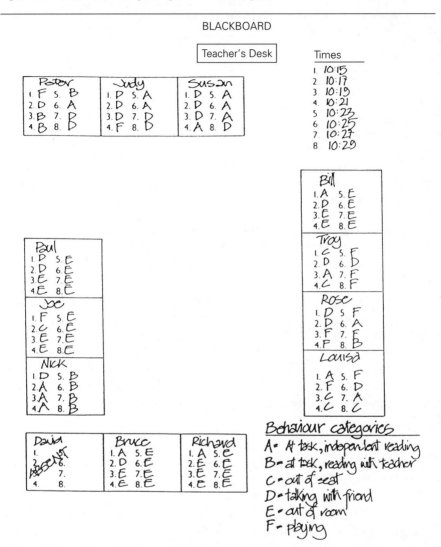

BLACKBOARD

Teacher's Desk

(*Source*: Adapted from K. Acheson and M. Gall (1980) *Techniques in The Clinical Supervision of Teachers*, Longman, New York, p. 110.)

In addition to producing a visual representation of the data that was collected from this observation, the teacher and her observer produced a tabular summary (*see* Table 2.3) of what emerged. This provided additional information for later discussion.

An analysis of this kind allows the teacher to focus on a range of important issues. For example:

Table 2.3   Recording student activity

Student Activity	10.15	10.17	10.19	10.21	10.23	10.25	10.27	10.29	Total	%
A At task, independent activity	4	1	2	2	2	4	2	0	17	18
B At task, reading with teacher	0	0	1	1	2	1	1	2	8	8
C Out of seat	1	1	1	2	0	0	0	0	6	6
D Talking to a friend	5	8	2	0	0	2	2	3	22	23
E Out of the room	0	1	5	5	5	5	5	5	31	32
F Playing	2	1	1	2	3	0	2	1	12	13

(*Source*: Acheson and Gall (1980) *op cit*)

1   Without passing judgment on whether it was 'good' or 'bad', attention might be directed to the relatively low levels of on task activity during this part of the lesson and consider why this was the case.
2   For a significant part of the lesson, a large number of students were absent from the classroom at the same time. Was the teacher conscious of this and what implications arise?
3   A very small proportion of the children appear to be receiving the teacher's attention. Why is this and what implications arise?
4   A significant number of children are either talking to friends or playing. Why is this so and what might be done to improve the situation?

The final example of diagrammatic procedures that can be used to synthesize classroom observations focuses on the teacher and attends to his or her movement around a classroom for a specific period of time. It provides interesting evidence of the amount of contact received by some children rather than others. Figure 2.5 relates to a traditional classroom structure, but it can be just as revealing in a more flexible classroom environment.

The most extreme example of structured observation is described as 'systematic observation'. These approaches tend to be employed in research projects and are based upon criteria that are carefully defined and highly specific, so that it is absolutely clear how the observations are to be undertaken and individual bias in perception and interpretation is eradicated. As a result, they tend to be undertaken by trained observers. The typical characteristics of systematic observation have been defined by Croll (1986) in the following way:

Figure 2.5   Observation using a diagram for recording (iv)

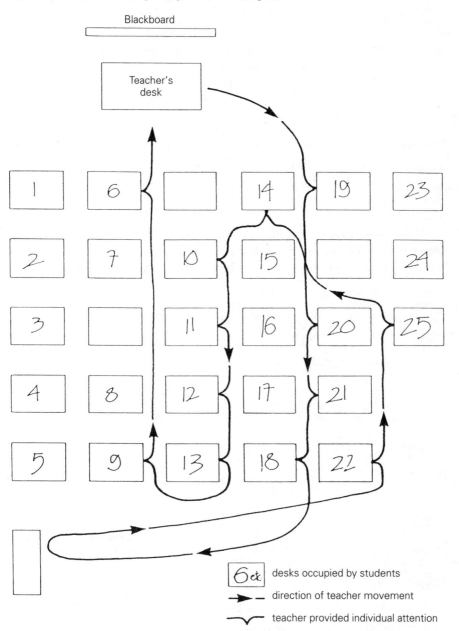

- It is explicit in its purpose or purposes, and these have to be worked out before data collection takes place.
- It is explicit and rigorous in its definition of categories and in its criteria for classifying phenomena into these categories.

- It produces data that can be presented in quantitative form and can be summarized and related to other data using statistical techniques.
- Once the procedures for recording and criteria for using categories have been arrived at, the role of the observer is essentially one of following instructions to the letter, and any other observer should record a particular event in an identical fashion to any other. (pp. 5–6)

Probably the most well known systematic observational procedure is that developed by Flanders (1972), which focuses on classroom language and explores his hypothesis that two-thirds of the time there is talk going on in classrooms, and two-thirds of the time that talk is teacher talk.

The observation schedule has clearly identified categories and explicit explanations for each of them. The process of data gathering is described by Hopkins (1993, pp. 109–10) in Table 2.4 below.

Table 2.4   Flanders's interaction analysis system

---

1. Every three seconds the observer writes down the category best describing the verbal behaviour of the teacher and class.

Teacher talk	1.	accepts feelings
	2.	praise
	3.	accepts ideas
	4.	question
	5.	lecture
	6.	command
	7.	criticism
Pupil talk	8.	solicited
	9.	unsolicited
	10.	silence

2. The numbers are written in sequence across the data sheet.
3. Each line of the data sheet contains twenty squares, thus representing approximately one minute of time.
4. Separate 'episodes' can be identified by scribbled margin notes, and a new line started for a new 'episode'.
5. In a research project the observer would have a pocket timer designed to give a signal every three seconds, thus reminding him or her to record a tally (a stop-watch or the secondhand of a wristwatch can be used).

(*Source*: Hopkins, 1993)

Another well-known example of a systematic observation procedure comes from the Oracle project that was based at the University of Leicester, 1979–82 (Galton, Simon and Croll, 1980). One of the directors of the project, Maurice Galton, accepts that

It's very difficult for an outside observer simply to come in with no previous knowledge or experience of a classroom and sit at the back of the room and make decisions associated with a prescribed set of categories. It requires an observer to go in on a number of occasions and begin to identify the patterns that exist, the typical ways of working. As a result, you begin to understand the ways in which the classroom works and the roles and responses of the individual children. (Galton, OU Course E364, video, 1983)

Table 2.5   The observation categories of the teacher's record in the Oracle Project

Conversation	Silence
Questions	silent interaction
Task	gesturing
Q1 recalling facts	showing
Q2 offering ideas, solutions (closed) Marking	
Q3 offering ideas, solutions (open) Waiting	
Task supervision	story
Q4 referring to task supervision	reading
Routine	not observed
Q5 referring to routine matter	not coded
Statements	no interaction
Task	adult interaction
S1 of facts	visiting pupil
S2 of ideas, problems	not interacting
Task supervision	out of room
S3 telling child what to do	
S4 praising work or effort	audience
S5 feedback on work or effort	composition
Routine	activity
S6 providing information, directions	
S7 providing feedback	
S8 of critical control	
S9 of small talk	

(*Source*: Galton, Simon and Croll, 1980)

The Oracle project used two main observation instruments, the 'Pupil Record' and the 'Teacher Record', details of which are shown in Tables 2.5 and 2.6. The Pupil Record was developed from an American observational schedule called PROSE (the Personal Record of School Experience) and modified to take into account features typical of the primary classroom in the UK. The categories came from general discussion and a consideration of the expectations of people about what goes on in classrooms. The roots of such procedures can be traced back to the ideas of Flanders. Hitchcock and Hughes (1989, p. 142) raise questions about the validity of such processes, however, and point to the importance of non-verbal elements of classrooms that are not attended to in the Oracle procedures and those similar to them. Features such as facial expression, eye movements and expressions are all important elements of inter-personal communication and the meaning and significance of events can often be determined as much through them as what

Table 2.6   The observation categories of the pupil record in the Oracle Project

Category	Item	Brief definition of item
Coding the pupil–adult categories		
1 *Target's role*	INIT	Target attempts to become focus of attention (not focus at previous signal)
	STAR	Target is focus of attention
	PART	Target in audience (no child is focus)
	LSWT	Target in audience (another child is focus)
2 *Interacting adult*	TCHR	Target interacts with teacher
	OBSR	Target interacts with observer
	OTHER	Target interacts with any other adult, such as the head or secretary
3 *Adult's interaction*	TK WK	Adult interacts about task work (task content or supervision)
	ROUTINE	Adult interacts about routine matter (classroom management and control)
	POS	Adult reacts positively to task work (praises)
	NEG	Adult reacts negatively to behaviour etc. (criticizes)
	IGN	Adult ignores attempted initiation
4 *Adult's communication setting*	IND ATT	Adult gives private individual attention to target pupil
	GROUP	Adult gives private attention to target's group
	CLASS	Adult interacts with whole class
	OTHER	Adult gives private attention to another child or group or does not interact
Coding the pupil–pupil categories		
5 *Target's role*	BGNS	Target successfully begins a new contact
	COOP	Target cooperates by responding to an initiation
	TRIES	Target unsuccessfully tries to initiate
	IGN	Target ignores attempted initiation
	SUST	Target sustains interaction
6 *Mode of interaction*	MTL	Non-verbal, mediated solely by materials
	CNTC	Non-verbal, mediated by physical contact or gesture (with or without materials)
	VRB	Verbal (with or without materials, physical contact or gesture)
7a *Task of other pupil(s)*	S TK	Same as target's task
	D TK	Different from target's task
7b *Sex and number of other pupil(s)*	SS	Target interacts privately with one pupil of same sex
	OS	Target interacts privately with one pupil of opposite sex
	SEV SS	Target interacts publicly with two or more pupils having same sex as target
	SEV OS	Target interacts publicly with two or more pupils, of whom one at least is of the opposite sex to the target

Table 2.6   (cont'd)

Category	Item	Brief definition of item
7c Base of other pupil(s)	OWN BS	From target's own base
	OTH BS	From another base

Coding the activity and location categories

Category	Item	Brief definition of item
8 Target's activity	COOP TK	Fully involved and cooperating on approved task work (e.g. reading)
	COOP R	Fully involved and cooperating on approved routine work (e.g. sharpening a pencil)
	DSTR	Non-involved and totally distracted from all work
	DSTR OBSR	Non-involved and totally distracted from all work by the observer
	DSRP	Non-involved and aggressively disrupting work of other pupil(s)
	HPLY	Non-involved and engaging in horseplay with other pupil(s)
	WAIT TCHR	Waiting to interact with the teacher
	CODS	Partially cooperating and partially distracted from approved work
	INT TCHR	Interested in teacher's activity or private interaction with other pupil(s)
	INT PUP	Interested in the work of other pupil(s)
	WOA	Working on an alternative activity which is not approved work
	RIS	Not coded because the target is responding to internal stimuli
	NOT OBS	Not coded because the target is not observed for some reason
	NOT LISTED	Not coded because the target's activity is not listed
9 Target's location	P IN	Target in base
	P OUT	Target out of base but not mobile
	P MOB	Target out of base and mobile
	P OUT RM	Target out of room
10 Teacher activity and location	T PRES	Teacher present with target through interaction or physical proximity
	T ELSE	Teacher privately interacting elsewhere with other pupil(s) or visitor
	T MNTR	Teacher not interacting but monitoring classroom activities
	T HSKP	Teacher not interacting but housekeeping
	T OUT RM	Teacher out of room

The target pupil's behaviour was coded at regular 25 second intervals using a method of multiple coding.
(*Source*: Galton, Simon and Croll, 1980)

is said or done. They also question whether the data generated by systematic observations present an accurate picture of the reality of the events they claim to be describing. How typical is the sample of behaviour? They also question whether the observer is actually capable of making accurate judgments and correct interpretations of utterances in the space of 25 seconds.

Despite these reservations, and provided they are borne in mind, it is certainly possible for teachers and schools to use procedures of this kind as part of a data-collecting strategy in school-based inquiries. An example of how teachers and headteachers might use systematic approaches to classroom observation is illustrated by the opportunity one teacher had to spend time in another teacher's class as a part of an In-service course (Drummond, 1993). The observer negotiated the focus with the teacher, who wanted to know more about two children in her class. The observer used timed observations and presented the analysis of his observations for one day (Table 2.7).

Table 2.7   Timed observation

	Kim	**Michael**
Breaks and Movement	1hr 28 mins	1hr 27 mins
Musical activities and rehearsal	1hr 27 mins	2hr 05 mins
Listening to teacher and general discussion	35 mins	19 mins
Queuing	19 mins	28 mins
Preparing for work and packing away	30 mins	17 mins
Mathematics	16 mins	25 mins
Handwriting	10 mins	3 mins
Reading workshop cards	22 mins	6 mins
Talking to the teacher	2 mins	4 mins

(*Source*: Drummond, 1993)

The observer concluded:

> One of the most striking features is the amount of one-to-one contact on each occasion. It had appeared from my initial observations that Michael took a far greater share of this contact time than Kim, but the difference in total is only two minutes (even so, this is twice the amount of time). What the table does not show is the number of occasions that went to make up this contact time. The two minutes of direct contact which Kim had, came from two occasions when she went to the teacher's desk to have something explained . . . The four minutes which Michael spent in direct contact with the teacher were made up of 15 occasions when he went for help, 5 occasions when he was reprimanded and 2 occasions when he was praised (i.e. 22 incidents in all). The longest of these lasted 40 seconds, and the shortest only 3 seconds . . . To speak to the teacher on those 15 occasions meant Michael queuing for 28 minutes over the day. For her 2 minutes of one-to-one contact, Kim had to queue for 19 minutes. (Drummond, 1993, pp. 35–36)

The study also raises a number of other useful questions which could be used to help the teacher develop her practice. For example:

Michael spent more time on musical activity – Why?
Michael spent less time listening to the teacher – Why?
What can be done about the amount of time spent queuing?
The amount of individual time received by each child was very limited. What can be done about it?

Of course in such situations one has to be very wary of over-burdening the teacher with guilt. The process has to be positive and aimed at improvement in a specific area at a time. The example above also raises an important question regarding the reliability of data generated by observation. Would we all have constructed a similar chart if we had observed in the classroom from which this data was gathered? Would tomorrow produce a similar picture?

Issues of perception, interpretation and judgment are central features of the observation process and we have to recognize that we never undertake observations in a vacuum, as Abercrombie (1969) has argued:

> What is being perceived depends not only on what is being looked at but on the state of the perceiver. (p. 27) ... We tend to think of ourselves as passively receiving information from the outside world, but this is far from the case; in the process of receiving information we interpret and judge (p. 29) ... When the thing we look at is sufficiently like the thing we expect to see, and easily fits our schema, our experience helps us to see. It is only when what we expect to see is not there that our schema lead us astray. (p. 33) ... we never come to an act of perception with an entirely blank mind, but are always in a state of preparedness or expectancy because of our past experience. (p. 63)

An excellent example of the extent to which we interpret the world through our own experience and our own expectations is provided by Harlen (1985):

> Observation is a process through which we come to take notice, to become conscious, of things and happenings. It can involve the use of any of the senses, alone or in combination. But taking in information by observation is not like soaking up water into a sponge. The senses do not absorb everything that there is; they function selectively, and the selection is influenced by existing ideas and expectations. Our

existing concepts and knowledge affect what we see, hear or feel. For instance, two people observing the same formation of clouds in the sky may observe quite different things about them. One, who knows little about clouds except that they block out the sun and bring rain, may see only their extent across the sky and their darkness. Another, who knows the significance of different features of clouds, may be able to report on their probable height, depth, direction of movement, changing formation and be able to predict further changes from these observations. (pp. 21–22)

She goes on to describe the well-known story of the vicar and the entomologist who are walking in the churchyard one pleasant, summer's evening. The choir are fervently practising in the vestry and their singing mingles with the noise of crickets and other early evening countryside sounds. The vicar comments enthusiastically about the delightful sound they were hearing. The entomologist agrees and adds, 'It's wonderful to think that it comes from their back legs.' Though the same physical sounds were available to them both, what each heard was different. They had selected from the available sounds and attended to those related to their interests and conceptual strengths. As Bassey (1995) has argued, we all perceive and construe the world in ways which are similar but not necessarily the same, so there can be different understandings of what is real. The implication of these comments is that we need to treat the data generated by our observations carefully, to check whether the interpretations we offer are justified. It was this concern that leads us to argue strongly for collaboration with others in the interpretation of such data. Another way of overcoming the problems associated with bias is to enrich and validate observations by undertaking follow-up interviews with those you have been observing. This leads us to the next way in to school-based inquiries.

2. Interviews

The interview is the most direct way of finding out why a person does something or what his beliefs or opinions are. Through observation of behaviour, inferences may be drawn about the reasons for a person's actions, but the interview enables the respondent to express his feelings or reasons directly and at whatever length he feels necessary. (Hook, 1985, p. 136)

Although it could be argued that the 'formality' of an interview is unnecessary in a primary school, where people interact regularly on a daily basis, there is evidence to suggest that many interactions in primary schools are not the kind that engage teachers in serious reflection. What an interview can offer is the opportunity for that sustained reflection on important issues facing a school. It also allows an opportunity for individual perspectives to be gathered, and for less dominant members of staff to offer their views. Similarly, there is growing evidence that children's perspectives are an important source of information about ways of improving schools. Interviews with children can therefore provide useful additional information for systematic inquiry into important school concerns. As suggested in the last section, the evidence provided by interviews can also validate and raise further questions about the findings derived from observation.

Hook (1985) believes that the value of discussion and interview is that they provide the opportunity for gathering information about knowledge, feelings and attitudes, expectations and intentions, and actions and reasons for these actions. An interview following a classroom observation is fundamentally important for the observer to check that the assumptions and interpretations he or she has made are justifiable.

Interviewing has been described as an art, a skilled technique that is developed over time and through practice. With increasing confidence, it becomes an adaptable means of gaining access to colleagues' and childrens' perceptions and understandings. Drever (1995, p. 1) argues that the process of interviewing provides factual information, evidence of preferences and opinions and allows the exploration in depth of experiences, motivations and reasoning. As a result it is an important means of coming to a broader understanding of aspects of school life and an important source of information for decision-making.

To be successful as an interviewer requires a range of skills. Hook (1985) for example lists the characteristics of successful interviews and interviewers as being purposeful, supportive, humorous, responsive, egalitarian and displaying qualities such as frankness, friendliness, rapport, trust, confidentiality, spontaneity, ease, courtesy and understanding. He adds:

> Successful interviewers are those with the flexibility, sensitivity, insight and intuition to be able to secure the maximum amount of information . . . but at the same time make the [interviewee] feel that the information he is giving is important and beneficial. (Hook, 1985, p. 136)

Interviews range across a continuum from the highly structured to the unstructured, or combine the qualities of these extremes by starting with a series of clearly defined questions and then on the basis of responses the interviewer may decide to probe and explore reasons for earlier answers. Conner (1991) describes five main kinds of interview that can be used in school-based inquiries.

The Structured or Standardized Interview

A predetermined set of questions is asked in a prescribed order. In this kind of interview there are no variations. The analysis allows for clear comparison between respondents. It is virtually the completion of a questionnaire in a face-to-face situation. This process can be useful in the early stages of a school-based inquiry, especially when it is important to establish a base line of information.

The Unstructured or Unstandardized Interview

An approach usually associated with counselling, guidance and clinical psychology, it is highly unlikely that this is a process that would be used in the kind of inquiries discussed in this book. There may be occasions, however, when the process is needed to explore a particular teacher's or child's anxieties to decide how they might best be helped. In fact many teachers feel that the skills of counselling are becoming of increasing importance in schools. Those with such skills argue that they are extremely specialized and would caution us against attempting to become 'amateur psychiatrists'.

The Non-directive Interview

This provides a context in which the course of questioning and the topics of conversation are largely governed by the interviewee. Again, it is unlikely that this procedure will be used extensively in school-based investigations other than at an exploratory stage.

The Focused Interview

Here attention is directed towards a particular topic or theme, and is regarded by many as the most appropriate strategy for school investigations. They focus on the identified topic and use time effectively. If carefully organized, interviewees come prepared to answer the previously negotiated questions.

The Conversational Interview

In the relaxed environment of the classroom, staffroom or playground, children and adults can offer telling insights about a school which it might be difficult or impossible to access by other means. We should not deny the importance of such opportunities and need to be open to the information produced in such contexts. What we do need to recognize, however, is that there may be ethical issues involved in how such information might be used. At all times it is important to consider the implications for those involved, as was discussed earlier.

As is suggested above, the success or failure of an interview depends on thorough preparation and a clear understanding of the topic being considered. Newson and Newson (1976) suggest:

> Although it will be clear that she has some sort of guide to work, to, the good interviewer will ask individual questions as if she had made them up at the moment because she really wanted to know the answers. The order of the questions is worked out precisely, so that the conversation will have both flow and a variety of pace; and this together with a sensitive use of pausing and hesitation, facial expression and tone of voice, allows the interviewer to maintain at least an appearance of spontaneity, naturalness and ease. (p. 34)

A central feature of the interview process are the questions that are to be used. Hook has identified two main types of question: **closed** or fixed choice, and **open-ended**. The closed question is probably the most regularly used and invites answers to very specific questions with no real room for reflection. Closed questions usually lead to responses such as yes/no, agree/disagree, and for/against. Open-ended questions, on the other hand, allow participants to take some control of the process and offer as much information as he or she wishes to offer. They also allow the interviewer the freedom to construct questions on the basis of the respondent's reply, within the interview framework. There are two types of open-ended questions, the 'probe' which pursues further information and the 'funnel' which starts broadly but progressively focuses down to the main inquiry.

Drawing on the work of Walker and Adelman (1975), Conner (1991) offers a number of useful suggestions about effective interviewing in school inquiries:

- Try to be a sympathetic, interested and attentive listener without taking an active role. In this way you convey that you value and appreciate the interviewee's opinion.
- Try to be neutral. Do not express your own opinion, and be careful to avoid feelings of surprise or disapproval at responses.
- Try to be at ease. If you are, it will be conveyed to the participant(s) and help them to relax.
- Try to be reassuring. Participants need to feel sure that they are not being tested or scrutinized and that their role is not to search out the answer that is in your head.
- Try to be careful in the way questions are phrased. Donaldson (1979) reminds us that even the youngest children are able to demonstrate considerable knowledge and understanding if we discuss with them in an appropriate context, using language which they understand and when they are clear about the purposes and intentions of the adult who is working with them.
- Try to listen. As Hook (1985) suggests, the ability to wait is important in interviewing, 'Wait time' has been found to influence the length and quality of responses to questions.
- Try to summarize at various stages in the interview. This helps the interviewer to focus carefully on what has been said and it allows the interviewee to add to what has been said, to correct misunderstandings and to agree or disagree with the interviewer's interpretation. (p. 88)

There has been an increasing tendency to involve children in the process of reflecting on the effectiveness of their school, their teachers and what contributes to improving standards in their learning. (See, for example, Ruddock et al., 1995; MacBeath, Boyd et al., 1997.) Lewis (1992) has argued that one of the most effective ways of interviewing children is to do this in groups, which she believes has several advantages over individual interviews. In particular, they help to reveal consensus views. They may also generate richer responses by allowing participants to challenge one another's views and they can be used to verify ideas gained by other means (for example, from observation) and as a result improve the reliability of the information base. There are difficulties, however, that require sensitivity and skill on the part of the interviewer.

Children may be unwilling to respond in a frank and honest manner to their teacher or to the headteacher. Often this is as much to do with the unfamiliarity of the experience as anything else. With practice and regular opportunities, and evidence that their comments are taken seriously and acted upon, children can become a very important source of information for the improvement of school practices. To overcome the potential difficulties involved, it is important to create an atmosphere in the school and in classrooms that welcomes difference of opinion and accepts it as opinion and not personal critique.

An alternative to interviewing by an insider is to use an external participant to undertake such discussions. The outsider could be another teacher, a parent or governor, or it could be someone not involved in the school in any way but who satisfies the criteria for effective interviewing described above. The use of an outsider was a technique employed in the Ford Teaching Project, where it was found that children were often prepared to express themselves more openly to outsiders. The project produced a variety of publications to support the processes of school-based inquiry. Of particular relevance were some of the comments that they offered related to interviewing children, many of which are relatively obvious, but easily transgressed. It could also be justifiably argued that they apply as much to adults as to children.

- Children often need help to express themselves. The interviewer should, however, be very careful in this situation. If too little help is given, the child may simply respond with monosyllabic answers or 'I don't know!' If too much help is given, the child may believe that you want a specific answer. You will end up by putting the words into the child's mouth and having the child agree with what you have to say, rather than offer their perspective. Their advice is: Give help, not direction.
- Children often respond with a 'don't know' reply in order to gain time to gather their thoughts. If you get a 'don't know' response, do not be in too much of a hurry to pass on to the next item. Wait patiently and expectantly for a short while. The child will probably then expand on the original statement.
- The interview should be conducted informally. Do not intimidate the child by referring constantly to clip-boards and notes. If the child believes he or she is being examined by you, you will only get the answers he or she expects that you want to hear; it then becomes a 'guess what's in teacher's mind exercise'.
- Try to adopt a neutral attitude throughout. Remember you are seeking their views, not wanting to impose yours.

- Make it clear to the child that you are interested only in what he or she thinks and phrase questions accordingly. For example, 'What do *you* think happened earlier?' rather than 'What happened earlier?'
- Be attentive to what the child is saying, even if the responses are being recorded. If the child gets the impression that you are not listening or are not interested in what he or she has to say, it is likely to impede responses.
- You should try to talk to children at an appropriate level, using language that they understand, without being patronizing.
- Children should not be laughed at or ridiculed. Incorrect answers should be taken seriously and not scorned. They can be a very important source of differences in understanding and have implications for future learning and teaching.
- Preferably, sensitive children should be interviewed on their own, to allow them the opportunity to represent their views and not be in competition with the more voluble members of the group.
- The interview should be lively and interesting to sustain involvement. The child must see that you are interested, as well as expecting them to be.
- If the interviewer is a stranger to the school, it is important that there is an introduction and a period of time for the children to relax and get to know this person.
- As in all things, courtesy and encouragement are essential. (Adapted from Forsyth and Wood, undated, pp. 14–15)

A further alternative to using an outsider is to use the children themselves to interview each other. Fielding (1998) has suggested that with the development of the necessary skills, pupils can gain access to evidence from other pupils that can be denied to teachers. Prisk (1987) also demonstrated that even the youngest children can participate seriously in investigation and debate in the absence of the teacher. She allowed a group of 6-year-olds to engage in a discussion without her presence. The conversation was recorded and the transcript of their conversation revealed how candid and honest children can be, producing unanticipated outcomes and unusual evidence.

Interviews can be very time-consuming. An alternative strategy is to use a questionnaire to gather opinions and, on the basis of the analysis, focus interviews on a sample of respondents or on those who offer particularly significant responses. The next section offers advice on the use of questionnaires in school-based inquiry.

3. Questionnaires

> The world is full of well-meaning people who believe that anyone
> who can write plain English and has a modicum of common sense can
> produce a questionnaire. (Oppenheim 1966, p. vii)

Using questionnaires as a means of collecting school-wide opinion about
an issue has a number of important advantages as a data-collecting
procedure in school-based inquiries. They are an efficient use of time,
they allow anonymity for those completing the questionnaire and they
are seen as being reliable because they employ the use of the same
questions for everyone. It is also the case that you can ensure that there
is a high rate of return and they can be used effectively with both adults
and children. There are disadvantages, though. The information collected by questionnaire is usually factual; it tends to describe what is
happening, or what someone thinks, rather than offering an explanation
as to why something is the case. As a result, the information will tend to
be basic, but at the same time useful as a means of establishing a core
of understanding and for raising potential differences and difficulties.

It is too often assumed that devising a questionnaire is a simple task;
unfortunately, this is far from the case. The time needed to produce a
clear, unambiguous questionnaire is often underestimated. Great care is
needed to ensure that the questions are going to produce the information that you need. If insufficient time is invested in its construction, the
usefulness of the information it produces is reduced. It is also important
to think about how you are going to analyse the results at the point of
construction in order to ensure that analysis is not excessively time-
consuming. With these words of warning, what advice is there about
effective questionnaire design? Cohen and Manion (1985, p. 103) suggest that an ideal questionnaire should possess the same qualities as a
good law. It should be clear and unambiguous and should ensure the
least chance of respondent uncertainty in the meaning of questions. They
also emphasize that since people's participation is voluntary, a questionnaire should attempt to engage and sustain their interest, encouraging
their cooperation and answers that are as near to the truth as possible.

Bell (1987) argues that you will only reach the stage of designing a
questionnaire after you have thoroughly explored the nature of your
inquiry.

> Only then will you know whether a questionnaire is suitable for the
> purpose and likely to yield usable data. Ask yourself whether a ques-
> tionnaire is likely to be a better way of collecting information than
> interviews or observation. (p. 58)

Munn and Drever (1991, p. 19) suggest that there are four essential principles in effective questionnaire design:

1 A questionnaire should be attractive to look at.
2 It should be brief.
3 It should be easy to understand.
4 It should be reasonably quick to complete.

At the heart of a good questionnaire are the questions around which it is composed. As Hitchcock and Hughes (1989) explain:

> Questions may structure responses too much or they may lead the respondent into answering in a particular way thus affecting the accuracy of the survey. Perhaps most important is the overall wording and presentation of a questionnaire. Is there ambiguity or vagueness in the questions? Might the presentation of the questions be offputting to certain respondents? How are questions dealing with sensitive areas worded and presented? The underlying assumption of . . . questionnaires is that people not only say what they mean but also do what they say. (p. 25)

Despite these concerns, there is a lot of useful advice regarding question design. For example, Cohen and Manion (1985) suggest that you should avoid **leading** questions, which are worded in such a way that it appears there is only one correct answer. **Complex** questions should also be avoided, as should **irritating** questions, for example:

> Have you ever attended an in-service course of any kind during your entire teaching career? If you are over 40 and have never attended an in-service course, put one tick in the box marked NEVER and another in the box marked OLD. (p. 107)

They also suggest that you should avoid **negative** questions and **open-ended** questions. The latter are regarded by Cohen and Manion as too demanding of most respondents' time. We would argue that open questions are very important because they provide the opportunity for explanation, which is very important in school investigations. The implication is to keep the questionnaire small and manageable, with a balance of open and specific questions. If there is a need for a predominantly open questionnaire, it is best to keep the number of questions to a maximum of about six, but with space for responses.

Youngman (1986) distinguishes between seven different types of questions.

1 **Verbal or open questions**
   The expected response is a word, phrase or extended comment. Responses to verbal questions can produce useful information but can cause problems in analysis, because of the different ways in which respondents can react to such questions.

2 **List questions**
   A list of alternatives is offered, any of which might be selected as the response.

3 **Category questions**
   The respondent is able to answer within one of a number of given categories (e.g. age ranges: 16–20, 21–25, 26–30; or type of class: Nursery/Reception, KS1, KS2, KS3, KS4, KS5).

4 **Ranking questions**
   The respondent is asked to place alternatives in rank order. For example, a question might invite someone to place qualities or characteristics (such as participation, individuality, collaboration, constructively critical) into an order of preference with the most important characteristic first.

5 **Scale questions**
   These invite respondents to offer a response on a scale from 'strongly agree' through 'neutral' to 'strongly disagree'.

6 **Quantity questions**
   This kind of question allows a response according to an amount of a characteristic. For example, 50% of time is spent on Maths or two-thirds of my working time is spent marking and planning.

7 **Grid questions**
   These lay out a framework for responses, often to more than one question. For example: How many years have you spent working with the following age ranges?

	1–2 years	3–4 years	5–6 years	more than 6 years
Infant				
Junior				
JMI				
First				
Middle				
First & Middle				

Bell (1987, pp. 60–63) draws attention to other important elements of question wording that need to be addressed in questionnaire design. She emphasizes the importance of avoiding **ambiguity**, **imprecision** and **assumption** in question wording. Words which have a common meaning to one person may mean something quite different to another. Bell offers the following example to illustrate the potential problems:

To what extent are you involved with the school curriculum? (Please tick)	A great deal ....
	A certain amount ....
	Not at all ....

Responses to a question like this can be very confusing for the respondent and for analysis. 'A great deal' may mean something very different for governor A than for governor B. Can we be sure that they interpret the word 'curriculum' in the same way? If a definition of the curriculum had been provided, then it would be possible to be confident about comparisons.

Bell also warns against questions which rely too heavily on **memory**. For example, if you were asked what subjects you studied at primary school, it is likely that you will remember some, but not all of the detail. Similarly, questions which rely on **knowledge** and ask for information that is not immediately available to the respondent can lead to a false answer, a guess or even ignoring that particular question. **Double questions** should also be avoided, other than in those described above as 'Grid' questions. Double questions include two alternatives in the same question. For example: Which do you prefer, football or rugby? What happens if you have no preference and enjoy each sport equally! Similarly you should avoid questions that presume a particular view or the possession of certain knowledge. You also need to beware of including hypothetical questions and those which are offensive or potentially sensitive. Bell (1988, pp. 67–69) provides a useful checklist of the stages of questionnaire design and construction that we have adapted for the purposes of school-based investigations. As you will see, there are two important stages *before* the decision to start constructing a questionnaire!

1 Decide what you want to know.
2 Ask yourself why you need this information.
3 Is a questionnaire the best way of obtaining this information?
4 If so, begin to draft some questions and in the process consider how the answers will be analysed.

5 Check the wording of the questions. (Is there any ambiguity, imprecision or assumption? Are you asking respondents to remember, or are you asking for knowledge they may not have? Have you included any double, leading, hypothetical or offensive questions?)
6 Decide on the most appropriate question type (verbal, list, category, scale, quantity or grid; each of these require different processes of analysis).
7 When you are satisfied that the questions are all well worded and in an appropriate format, order them.
8 Write out the instructions for the completion of the questionnaire.
9 Consider the layout and appearance.
10 Produce a final draft.
11 Pilot the questionnaire.
12 Make adjustments in the light of reactions.
13 Produce sufficient copies of the final version for distribution and set a fixed timescale for return.
14 Analyse the responses.
15 Produce a summary for sharing with colleagues!

The following questionnaires provide an illustration of the way in which they can be used with colleagues, parents, governors and children for the improvement of schools. It also offers examples of procedures that can be used and adapted for school inquiries. It is not always necessary to produce your own questionnaire. If one is available that satisfies your area of concern, as was suggested earlier with reference to projects like the GRIDS project, use it.

The first questionnaire (Questionnaire 1) was produced by a group of teachers involved in the Ford Teaching Project (Browning, undated), who were involved in investigating 9–12-year-olds' experience of learning. Their first questionnaire was quite simple and straightforward and, as was suggested above, they produced an analysis sheet for the questionnaire. A later example of the questionnaire (Questionnaire 2) built on their experience of piloting the first questionnaire and produced a second version, which appears more complex, but evidence suggested that the children found the second version easier to follow and complete. As Walker (1985) suggests, this is the reverse of what normally happens with questionnaires. 'In the process of testing they usually become shorter and simpler as ambiguity and open questions are monitored and removed' (p. 94).

A second illustration of questionnaires that have been used to explore aspects of schools comes from the NUT-commissioned framework

Managing Improving Primary Schools

Questionnaire 1

Name ....
Date ....
Please try to give an answer to all the questions. Underline the answer you think applies.

1. Did you learn anything new?

   nothing/a little/some/a fair amount/a lot

2. Did you find the session interesting?

   interesting/acceptable/boring

   Can you give a reason? ....

3. Did you understand what you were supposed to do?

   fully/sufficiently/vaguely/not at all

4. Did the teacher talk?

   too much/enough/too little

5. Did you need any help from the teacher?

   none/a little/some/a fair amount/a lot

6. Were you able to get the help you needed from the teacher?

   straight away/after a little while/after some time/after a long time

   If you had to wait for help, or never got help, can you give a reason? ....

7. Did you ask for help from outside your group?

   frequently/occasionally/not at all

8. Could you find all the things you needed?

   all of them/most of them/some of them/a few of them/none of them

9. Were you interrupted by other people outside your group?

   frequently/occasionally/not at all

10. If you were delayed, was it caused by . . . ?

    *going out/unable to talk to teacher/someone coming into the room/
    unable to concentrate/lack of equipment/any other reason*

Here is a space for you to write any other comments about the session. You may continue on the other side if you wish.

Analysis Sheet for Questionnaire 1

1. Did you learn anything new?

nothing	a little	some	a fair amount	a lot

2. Did you find the session interesting?

interesting	acceptable	boring

3. Did you understand what you were supposed to do?

fully	sufficiently	vaguely	not at all

4. Did the teacher talk?

too much	enough	too little

5. Did you need any help from teacher?

none	a little	some	a fair amount	a lot

6. Were you able to get the help you needed from the teacher?

straight away	after a little while	after some time	after a long time

7. Did you ask for help from outside your group?

frequently	occasionally	not at all

8. Could you find all the things you needed?

all of them	most of them	some of them	a few of them	none of them

9. Were you interrupted by other people outside your group?

frequently	occasionally	not at all

10. If you were delayed, was it caused by . . . ?

going out	unable to talk to teacher	someone coming into the room
unable to concentrate	lack of equipment	any other reason

(*Source*: Browning et al., n.d., pp. 6, 7)

for self-evaluation (MacBeath, Boyd et al., 1997). Three questionnaires were produced for this study, which was based upon the views from ten schools in Scotland and the different perspectives of over 630 people representing teachers, management, support staff, pupils, parents and governors. The three questionnaires relate to different areas of school life. The first questionnaire (Questionnaire 3) collects information related to 'support for teaching', and is aimed primarily at the teachers. The second questionnaire (Questionnaire 4) contains questions about 'school climate' and can be used with pupils, teachers, management, governors and parents, as can the third questionnaire (Questionnaire 5), which is based upon what pupils in the study said about good teachers.

Another example of a useful questionnaire that investigates the climate of a school comes from a project undertaken at the University of Cambridge Institute of Education that developed a variety of procedures for gaining access to characteristics of schools. The example shown (Questionnaire 6) provides a means by which the 'climate' of a school can be identified. It focuses on everybody's perception of the quality

Questionnaire 2   An extract from the second questionnaire from the Ford Teaching Project to illustrate the change in structure following piloting

Name ....   Subject ....
Date ....
Please answer all the questions by marking in the appropriate 'box'.

1. Did you learn anything new?

nothing	a little	some	a fair amount	a lot

Was this because you were recording (writing up, etc.) your discoveries?

yes	no

→ Give a reason why you think you didn't learn anything new

2. Did you find the session:

very interesting	interesting	acceptable	boring

Give your reasons

Was this because you were recording (writing up, etc.) your findings?

yes	no

How did you record your discoveries?

Please give your reasons why you found this session boring

3. Did you notice any difference about the session?

yes	no

What difference?

Section from Analysis Chart A for Questionnaire 2

2. Did you find the session \ 1. Did you learn anything new?	nothing	a little	some	a fair amount	a lot
very interesting					
interesting					
acceptable					
boring					

(*Source*: Browning et al., n.d., pp. 11–17)

Questionnaire 3

SUPPORT FOR TEACHING	strongly agree	agree	disagree	strongly disagree
The size of classes ensures that effective teaching can take place				
School management is aware of what goes on in classrooms				
Bad behaviour is dealt with effectively				
Support for learning and teaching is at the heart of school policy and planning				
Parents support their children's learning				
Pupils show respect for teachers, time is given to things that are important				
There is an adequate level of resources for teaching purposes				
Staff respect one another's work				
Workload is distributed fairly among staff				
There is a strong common sense of purpose and direction among staff				
The headteacher is accessible				
Staff share problems in their teaching				
Achievements of teachers are recognized and rewarded				
Management takes time to listen to teachers' concerns				

(*Source*: MacBeath et al., 1997)

Questionnaire 4

THE SCHOOL	a lot like this school	quite like this school	not much like this school	not at all like this school
The school is a safe place				
Pupils and teachers respect one another				
Visitors feel welcome in the school				
The school is well thought of in the community				
There is large amount of vandalism and graffiti				
Class sizes ensure that pupils get individual attention				
Pupils are well behaved and well mannered				
The school is willing to change and adapt the way it does things				
There is a broad and varied curriculum catering to a wide range of needs				
Pupils get help and support when they need it. There is good leadership				
There is a good overall level of attendance				
All pupils are encouraged to reach their maximum potential				
Most pupils enjoy coming to the school				
Most teachers enjoy coming to the school				

(*Source*: MacBeath et al., 1997)

Questionnaire 5

TEACHERS	true of nearly all teachers	true of most teachers	true of some teachers	true of only a few teachers
like teaching				
treat people equally				
let pupils know how they are doing				
are encouraging				
make their subject interesting				
listen to the opinions of young people				
make allowances for pupils with problems				
take time to explain things				
don't give up on you				
know how to help you when you don't understand the work				
keep confidences				
help you to feel self-confident				
expect you to work hard and do well				

(*Source*: MacBeath et al., 1997)

and extent of enquiry and reflection, planning, involvement, staff development, coordination and leadership in the school and can be a useful means of stimulating discussion and school development. The fact that the analysis allows differentiation between the 'management' of a school, teachers and support staff allows analysis by sub-group as well as the whole school. The results assess a school's development structure and provides evidence of 'readiness for change'. The technique can be used to map changes in a school's climate over time, as a diagnostic

Questionnaire 6   This gathers evidence on the following areas: the extent of inquiry reflection; the effectiveness of planning; involvement in decision-making; opportunities for staff development; coordination and leadership. Three elements of the questionnaire are illustrated below.

INQUIRY/REFLECTION				
1.1	**In this school we talk about the quality of our teaching**			
	RARELY	SOMETIMES	OFTEN	NEARLY ALWAYS
1.2	**As a school we review the progress of changes we introduce**			
	RARELY	SOMETIMES	OFTEN	NEARLY ALWAYS
1.3	**Teachers make time to review their classroom practice**			
	RARELY	SOMETIMES	OFTEN	NEARLY ALWAYS
1.4	**The school takes care over issues of confidentiality**			
	RARELY	SOMETIMES	OFTEN	NEARLY ALWAYS
COORDINATION				
5.1	**Staff taking on coordinating roles are skilful in working with colleagues**			
	RARELY	SOMETIMES	OFTEN	NEARLY ALWAYS
5.2	**We get tasks done by working in teams**			
	RARELY	SOMETIMES	OFTEN	NEARLY ALWAYS
5.3	**Staff are kept informed about key decisions**			
	RARELY	SOMETIMES	OFTEN	NEARLY ALWAYS
5.4	**We share experiences about the improvement of classroom practice**			
	RARELY	SOMETIMES	OFTEN	NEARLY ALWAYS
LEADERSHIP				
6.1	**Staff in the school have a clear vision of where we are going**			
	RARELY	SOMETIMES	OFTEN	NEARLY ALWAYS
6.2	**Senior staff delegate difficult and challenging tasks**			
	RARELY	SOMETIMES	OFTEN	NEARLY ALWAYS
6.3	**Senior management take a lead over development priorities**			
	RARELY	SOMETIMES	OFTEN	NEARLY ALWAYS
6.4	**Staff are given opportunities to take on leadership roles**			
	RARELY	SOMETIMES	OFTEN	NEARLY ALWAYS

(*Source*: Ainscow et al., 1994)

instrument to ascertain differences in perceptions between different staff groups and to make comparisons between schools. It has been a very effective strategy employed in the Essex Primary Schools Initiative, a primary school improvement project (Southworth, 1997).

The final examples of questionnaires illustrate ways in which the perspectives of children might be obtained. Hopkins (1993) suggests that with younger children it is probably more effective to use relatively simple questions with easy-to-answer procedures. He advocates the use of 'smiley' faces or cartoon features, as is illustrated in Question-naire 7. The advantage of this kind of questionnaire is that it is easy and fun to complete and can provide potential avenues for follow-up with the children at a later stage, probably by interview or group discussion. Properly constructed, they can provide a teacher and the school with information about individuals and groups on a variety of themes, and are a particularly pertinent means of gaining access to children's feel-ings about their school experience, their learning and their progress.

The benefits to school improvement of using questionnaires of this kind with children is also illustrated by Dudley (1999). As part of an LEA school improvement initiative in Essex, a Learning Perception Sur-vey has been developed that invites children to offer their reaction to important issues related to their experience of schools. It is similar to those developed by the University of Keele (1994), and employs a questionnaire format for older children and a 'smiley face' response format for use with younger children (Questionnaires 8 and 9). As Barber et al. (1994) comment, 'These instruments have now been used in a wide range of schools nation-wide. There is growing demand for them across the country' (p. 8).

A further interesting development related to Dudley's work is that he has followed up teachers' reactions to the analysis of their children's responses when compared to an anonymous group of 'like' schools. What was particularly significant was that when responses were posit-ive most teachers took it as evidence of the success of their practice. When responses were more critical and their school appeared not to be competing successfully with comparative schools, teachers tended to criticize the questionnaire. As a result he raises questions about teachers' skills of interpreting data. This is an issue which is discussed in a later section.

The next useful source of information that can be used to stimulate inquiries and contribute to more effective management is to subject your documentation to regular scrutiny. Documentary analysis is considered in the next section.

Questionnaire 7   Reading Attitude Survey

NAME _____   ROOM _____   TEACHER _____

1. How do you feel when your teacher reads a story aloud?

2. How do you feel when someone gives you a book for a present?

3. How do you feel about reading books for fun at home?

4. How do you feel when you are asked to read aloud to your group?

5. How do you feel when you are asked to read aloud to your teacher?

(*Source*: Hopkins, 1993)

Questionnaire 8   The Learning Perception Survey
(Extract from the 'early years' version)

1. When you get up in the morning do you look forward to going to school?

Yes   No

(*Source*: Essex LEA)

3. Does your teacher usually have time to listen to your questions?

Yes   No

Questionnaire 9   The Learning Perception Survey (after Essex LEA)
(Illustration from the older children's version)

Instructions – How to answer the questions

Please pick a box which is closest to how you feel

e.g. Do you enjoy reading?
If you **really** enjoy reading, colour in box no 4

If you **like it a bit**, colour in box 3

If you **don't like it much**, colour in box 2

If you **don't like it at all**, colour in box 1

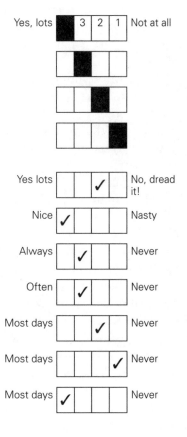

<u>Start here</u>

1. When you get up, do you look forward to going to school?

2. Are the older children in the school nice to younger children about their work?

3. Does your teacher usually have time to listen to your questions?

4. When you are at home do you sometimes think of things to tell your teacher about?

5. When you are at home do you talk about what you have been doing at school?

6. Do you read to someone at home?

7. Do you read to yourself at home?

(*Source*: Essex LEA)

4. Documentary Analysis

> Once a written source has been created . . . it becomes a 'potential' historical fact and therefore documentary data. For example, minutes of a school committee meeting, or guidelines issued by a school to parents . . . they all say something about the school. (Hitchcock and Hughes, 1989, p. 124)

If there is one thing that the 1988 Education Act and its associated school inspection regime has done, it has ensured that schools are buried under a mountain of documentation. A regular gripe at in-service courses is often related to impending Ofsted inspections and the implications this has for checking the paperwork! Reflecting on the past paperwork produced by a school can be a useful source of questions about practice. For example, we believe that statements of school aims should always be seen as a working document and as the basis of a great deal of decision-making that goes on in a school. When planning a unit of work, the school aims should inform the plan. Similarly, when evaluating a unit of work, the school aims should provide a useful evaluation checklist. 'Has what we did contributed to the achievement of any of the aims? If not, why not?'

Too often in the recent past the production of documentation has been seen as a chore to satisfy external audiences rather than to establish principles for practice within a school. It is also the case that when considering the production of a new document, we tend to start anew, rather than basing it on an evaluation of what was effective in the past. Documentary analysis, therefore, should be part and parcel of a school's development.

The analysis of the detail of school documents has a number of advantages, especially for external audiences because they provide evidence of the espoused principles of a school's practice. They also provide evidence of the way in which the curriculum is interpreted and likely to be enacted. It is important, therefore, that you reflect on the way in which a document produced by the school may be interpreted by an outside audience. This is why spending some time looking at your documentation is time well spent.

An example discussed in section 3, describes a school that was unhappy about some of the elements of their Ofsted report and where further observation by an external observer provided evidence to support and critique the Ofsted findings. One aspect of the review had been a critical scrutiny of their documentation. This was where the main weakness lay. The description of the organization and structure of the criticized area of the curriculum was difficult to understand. As a result of the review, that part of their curriculum explanation was rewritten and included the views of pupils and parents as well as teachers. They also invited a variety of other people to read the documentation to see if it made sense.

5. The Analysis of Assessment Information

The most recent demand placed upon schools concerns the analysis of assessment-related information. This has become particularly significant with the imposition of targets for literacy and numeracy. It will be impossible to set targets that are **S**pecific, **M**easurable, **A**chievable, **R**ealistic and **T**ime-related (i.e. **SMART**) without engaging in the processes of data collection and analysis that have been discussed so far. The importance of target-setting within the current government's strategy for education is reflected in a comment in the White Paper on Education *Excellence in Schools* (1997) where it was argued:

> The use within schools of reliable and consistent performance analyses enables teachers to assess progress by their pupils and to change their teaching strategies accordingly. Comparisons of performance by different subjects, classes, year-groups and other categories help schools to set targets for individual pupils which take full account of each pupil's starting points. Such detailed comparisons also help head teachers to monitor the performance of classroom teachers. (paragraph 3.15)

In response to the question 'Why set targets?', the DfEE Standards and Effectiveness Unit (DfEE, 1997b) suggested that:

> Target-setting leads to greater clarity and helps a school focus on pupil performance. Head teachers can use pupil performance targets to underline priorities and serve as a reminder of where the school is heading. Target-setting also aids school review. Pupil performance targets provide firm evidence against which to judge recent progress. With pupil performance targets, head teachers and governing bodies can see more clearly whether they are achieving or falling short in their main goals. This should lead them to identify the approaches to improvement which work. (p. 6)

In a publication produced in 1996 (DfEE/Ofsted), it was argued that the best practice in target-setting is based upon self-critical reflection and analysis of the school's performance. All available data should be used to review and monitor past performance and to predict potential performance so that effort and resources can be focused on pupils who are under-achieving or being insufficiently challenged. It was emphasized that target-setting needs to be precisely planned, focused on improvement which is attainable and measurable and broken down to a level that allows individual teachers to take responsibility for setting and achieving targets. In a later publication (DfEE, 1997b) a process for target-setting is defined. The procedure that is suggested is very similar to those described earlier, in that it is framed around a series of questions. For target-setting, the process has been described as the '5 stage cycle of school improvement'.

Stage 1 **How well are we doing?** This focuses attention on an analysis of the school's current performance by looking critically at pupils' achievements.

Stage 2 **How well should we be doing?** To answer this question, schools need to compare current and previous results and those from similar schools using benchmark information.

Stage 3 **What more can we achieve?** The analysis which results from stages 1 and 2 provides the information for schools to set clear and measurable targets for improvement.

Stage 4 **What must we do to make it happen?** At this stage the school development plan is reconsidered and actions identified to make sure targets are achieved.

Stage 5 **Take action, review successes and start the cycle again.** As a result of the evaluation of the effectiveness of strategies to achieve the targets set, the process starts again and reinforces the importance of monitoring and evaluation for improvements to pupil performance and the standards achieved by the school.

In developing advice for the schools in their authority, LEA advisers in Birmingham have produced a series of supplementary questions, all of which are dependent on the collection and careful analysis of evidence.

- Are we doing as well as we should with all our pupils?
- What more should we aim to achieve this year?
- How does performance in our school compare with national standards?

- How does performance in our school compare with the LEA as a whole?
- Are we doing as well as schools with a similar intake?
- Do we have any significant weaknesses in attainment in particular aspects of the curriculum?
- Are there particular groups of pupils on whom we should target our improvement efforts?
- At what level should we be setting targets for the core subjects?
- At what level should we be setting targets for end of key stage assessments?
- At what level should our targets be for particular year-groups, classes, groups of pupils, individual pupils?
- What process targets should we be setting to develop our whole school systems and procedures for managing improvement?

It is also emphasized that thought needs to be given to who should be involved in the collection of the evidence related to each of these questions: subject leaders, class teachers, pupils, governors, parents? Whoever is involved, the main aim should be 'to improve on our previous best'. As a previous DES document on target-setting has suggested (DfEE/Ofsted), 'Setting targets makes you focus on what children are actually learning, not what you think you are teaching' (front page).

Targets have been defined in a variety of ways. For example, the DfEE (1997) offers an illustration from one school that defines targets in terms of anticipated percentage increases:

- to increase the percentage of children attaining level 2 in reading by 5%
- to increase the percentage of children reaching level 3 in reading by 2%
- to increase the percentage of children leaving Reception knowing 23 or more letter sounds by an average of 20%

In their advice to schools about target-setting, the London region of the Association of Advisers and Inspectors for Assessment (1998) distinguish between 'learning' targets and 'attainment or progress' targets, as can be seen in Table 2.8.

In their advice to their schools, Essex LEA has distinguished between **Outcome Targets**, which are related to a percentage of pupils achieving at or above expected levels in the National Curriculum core subjects, **Progress Targets**, which are concerned with the progress pupils make compared to their prior attainment in the three core subjects,

Table 2.8   Types of target

Focus	Type of target	Example
Individual pupils	• learning	• to use phonic cues in addition to picture cues when reading
	• attainment/progress	• to achieve level 4 by the end of the key stage
Class or year groups	• learning	• to be able to use full stops accurately
	• attainment/progress	• X% at level Y at the end of the year
School	• attainment/progress	• average reading age to increase by 3% this year

(*Source*: London AAIA, 1998)

Table 2.9   Outcome, process and learning targets

Target	Whole School	Class, year or group of pupils	Individual pupils
Outcome Targets	Improving the % of pupils achieving level 4 by the end of KS2. Reduce the % of pupils graded W at the end of KS1 to zero	Move the three pupils on stage 3 of the Special Needs register in class 3 with reading targets back down to stage 2	Personal improvement in reading age or reaching a specific objective on the LEA reading profile
Progress Targets	Increase the progress in English at KS2 by 0.4 of a level from an average of 1.6 (1993–97) to an average level of 2.0 (1995–99)	Increase the % of pupils in Y3 reading at or above their chronological age from 55% to 75% during the year	To know an additional 15 key words by the end of the Spring term. Each pupil to have mental recall of multiplication facts 6×6 to 10×10
Learning	Improve proportion of children able to draft and redraft a story using a word-processor	Increase the proportion of Y6 pupils able to apply the skills of independent learning from 50% to 60%	Improve the skills of the six most able pupils in class 5 in self-assessment of Science Investigations

(*Source*: Essex LEA)

and **Learning Targets**, which are related to aspects of learning, for example the development of study skills and improvements in attitudes and motivation. These are illustrated in Table 2.9.

Schools that have attempted the process of target-setting have not necessarily found it easy. For example, in a report produced for the DfEE (Conner et al., 1998) some of the difficulties mentioned included:

- the fact that as a process it was very time-consuming
- that it was difficult to make targets challenging, meaningful, manageable and measurable

- that prioritizing was problematic, especially if more than one area of weakness had been identified
- setting realistic percentage improvements was difficult, as was defining exactly the level of improvement 'wanted' or 'needed'
- it was difficult to involve all children, targeting their individual needs
- being sufficiently specific about a target was also a problem, so that achievement could be recognized
- it was recognized that there is a need to handle some issues with great sensitivity, especially when the school weakness pointed to a particular member of staff underachieving
- the data upon which analysis is based is still relatively crude and focuses on a very narrow range of achievements

In order to overcome some of the concerns identified above, Southworth (1998) offers the following advice.

Handle Information with Care

If collecting data needs some thought, handling it needs even greater care. In primary schools, with their traditions of class teaching, data sets can often be related to specific class groups and thus to class teachers. This can mean that while the head is trying to develop a whole-school perspective and identify trends across the school, individual teachers are reading the same data to see how the information reflects on them. Data handling needs to avoid creating the circumstances where staff feel threatened and become defensive. It does not mean, however, that poor and ineffective teaching can be excused. As Southworth argues

> In short, data handling has its health hazards. The psychological health of teachers needs to be borne in mind and interpersonal sensitivities respected. This is not to sweep things under the carpet, nor to say that tough-minded analyses should not take place. It is, however, to recognise that those people who identify and agree the targets are also the same people who have to work to achieve them. If target-setting results in some staff feeling unable or demotivated to accomplish them, then the medium of target-setting is giving out the wrong messages. As one head said, 'I take the view that team issues are shared with the team and any individual issues with the individual.' (p. 134)

Do Not Be Too Respectful of the Information

Handling data is also made difficult because already there are signs that it is introducing its own pseudo-scientific language with the assumption that all that matters is statistics. Often the jargon and numbers associated with elements of the process of analysis inhibits understanding rather than promotes it. However, analysing the numerical and quantitative data related to target-setting should enable schools to detect issues that can then be focused upon. This is one of the lessons emerging from schools that have begun to use data for target-setting. The data highlights that 'something is going on here', or it acts as a 'can opener', lifting the lid on something which needs to be investigated. Data can help measure progress and achievement and help staff to identify areas of potential growth and to recognize success. Phil Hewett, a primary headteacher (in Conner, 1999) reinforces this when he says,

> I freely admit that it is only during the last six years that I have become a convert to the need for gathering and analysing the quantity of data that I now use for assessing the school's performance. When I first received a request from the government to complete a complicated and lengthy return about school attendance rates for the school year . . . I was extremely annoyed. However, once completed I was shocked to learn that we had a 9.7% absence rate. This was only just short of the Ofsted indicator for a failing school. The LEA average was 5.7% and the local average 6.5%. We set ourselves the target of reducing absence to the level of the local area. (p. 74–5)

Aim for Specific Targets

Southworth suggests that it is important to be as precise as possible in the definition of targets

> Try to be precise in how targets are framed and articulated. This is where benchmarking can help. If we can compare our school's performance in reading against another school which serves a similar pupil population, and find that they are apparently doing better than we are, then we have some grounds for acknowledging we need to improve. (p. 134)

This often leads staff to ask how much do they need their children to improve. If in a school reading ages are generally below chronological age by six months, whereas another school in similar circumstances has children whose reading ages regularly exceed their chronological age by three months, then the tendency for senior managers is to set a target, 'to increase children's progress so that their reading ages exceed chronological ages'. However, experience suggests that whilst this may be a laudable target, it may also be too imprecise and raises a number of questions, the first of which is when will this be achieved by? It may be more realistic to set such a target for two years hence, rather than to try to accomplish it within a single school year. On the other hand, three years may be too slow!

The next important question concerns the frequency by which pupil's reading ages are to exceed their chronological age. Is it good enough for some of the children or should all children satisfy the target? Does account need to be taken of summer-born children, or those with learning difficulties? Further precision in the wording of the target is essential. This makes analysis of achievements related to that target easier.

Targeted Action Matters

Once targets have been identified and agreed, there needs to be targeted action. Action plans should be carefully devised to help everyone realize the goals that have been set. Mechanisms need to be put in place to monitor progress and ensure that there are feedback sessions when findings about progress can be presented and discussed. The skills of school-based inquiry are essential for this process.

Target Learning, Develop Teaching

Teachers may need to change elements of their teaching, to achieve the targets that they set for themselves. One danger is that teachers will respond to the demands of target-setting by working harder and more intensively. In some situations this will lead to improvements, but targets should also increase the school's and teachers' effectiveness. Therefore, teachers may need to refine their practice, adopt new teaching strategies, or give different 'weight' to parts of their teaching. This will need to be supported.

Monitor the Targets Set

There is a symmetry to target-setting. Data analysis provides a starting point for generating targets and once they have been set, they must be monitored to check how much progress is being made towards reaching them, as well as providing evidence as to whether and how they have been met.

Targets Need to Be Communicated

For the process to be effective, a whole range of people need to be involved.

Children

Target-setting is most effective when it takes place within an information network that enables children to understand their levels of achievement, to set targets for their own learning and where they understand what they have to do next.

Teachers

Teachers need to assess children accurately within the context of whole-school agreed processes, advise them about achievable targets, set appropriate levels of work and provide regular and frequent feedback about progress towards the achievement of the targets. The regular process of review may lead to modification in the targets set.

Parents

Parents need to understand their children's levels of achievement, support and encourage target achievement and ensure set work is finished on time. There is evidence to suggest that parents are currently the least involved in the target-setting process (Conner, 1999).

Managers

Managers in a school should develop systematic whole-school approaches, relate targets to the school development plan, provide necessary support and resources, keep parents and governors informed and monitor the achievement of targets.

Governors

Governors have a responsibility to ensure that targets are included in the school development plan, that achievement of targets is evaluated, and to take action if targets are not being achieved. Again, evidence suggests that governor involvement tends to be limited (Conner, Dudley et al., 1999).

LEA

The LEA should provide benchmarking data and guidance to all of its schools to supplement that provided by the government and encourage the development of targets in each school.

Southworth concludes by reviewing some of the lessons that have been learned from schools involved in the early stages of target-setting.

1   Schools that have been involved suggest that targets should be measurable, pupil-driven, achievable but challenging.
2   Targets need to be differentiated for individual children, different groups, different subject areas and for the school as a whole.
3   In the early stages of writing targets it is important to share them outside the school and invite constructive critique.
4   Targets need to be monitored and the information used to help refine and develop subsequent targets.
5   Colleagues' classroom practices should be supported and developed. This can only come through effective strategies for monitoring.

Hewett (1999) supports each of these principles and emphasizes the importance of placing target-setting in the context of wider school improvement initiatives. He also reminds us that making 'significant, sound, sustained educational progress is, in athletics terms, more like being a long distance runner than a sprinter'. Success in target-setting, he suggests, should be judged by 'how close' a school gets to its targets, not always the expectation of achievement or exceeding them. Success should also be interpreted against the previous performance of the particular group for whom the target was set.

The evidence suggests that schools which use targets as part of a systematic and structured approach to school improvement find that teachers improve their knowledge and understanding of children's attainment and progress and by implication feel a greater sense of professional success. Through targeting, lessons are more clearly focused and related to learning objectives and children feel more confident about the expectations that are placed upon them. Southworth suggests that the central emphasis within the target-setting process is on effective school self-evaluation, a theme emphasized by Ofsted in their publication *School Evaluation Matters* (Ofsted, 1998), which argues for the importance of monitoring and evaluation based upon the analysis of assessment results. In a study of 100 primary and secondary schools, Ofsted (1998) found that schools appear to have a reasonably accurate idea of their strengths, but much less insight into their weaknesses. In the primary schools involved in this survey, only a small proportion of the school's weaknesses had been identified in the school development plan. As a result it is argued that schools need to develop their expertise in school-based evaluation. The main sources of evidence that it is suggested should be drawn upon include the results of assessments, tests and other examination results. In addition the PANDA (Performance and Assessment Report) produced for each school by Ofsted is recommended, as is comparative performance data now provided for their schools by many LEAs. The Ofsted evaluation report provides a guide to self-evaluation based upon the Ofsted framework for the inspection of schools. Not surprisingly, the introduction argues, 'To be efficient, effective and complementary, evaluation by the school should draw from the criteria and indicators used in inspection, and should employ similar techniques.'

Four main questions serve as the basis of the advice that is offered:

1 **How good is our school?** This question focuses on the outcomes of the education provided by a school, the standards achieved, the progress pupils make, their attitudes, behaviour and personal development and whether they come to school regularly and on time.

2 **What are our strengths and weaknesses?** Involves diagnosing why the school achieves what it does, by appraising the work of the school through observation and the collection of other relevant information.

3 **What must we do to improve?** Is concerned with how the results of evaluation are used to improve the standards and quality of teaching and learning in the school.

4 **Have we got what it takes?** Relates to the quality of leadership and management in a school and the skill and commitment of the staff to pursue improvement.

The report concludes that schools committed to improvement **monitor** performance at all levels in their school, **analyse** whether standards are high enough throughout the school using comparative data from similar schools, **evaluate** the quality of teaching and learning against national criteria, **plan** what needs to be done to overcome weaknesses, **set** clear objectives and targets for improvement, and **act** on the findings of monitoring, evaluation and diagnosis to promote more effective teaching and learning through support and training (p. 11).

Dudley (1999) has argued that for the above to be achieved, further consideration needs to be given to developing teachers' skills of the management, analysis, presentation and discussion of data and that, 'Data is a word with which many teachers feel uncomfortable . . . it conjures up in peoples' minds . . . numbers, computers, graphs, confusion and, of course . . . *Star Trek*!'

He goes on to emphasize the importance of seeing data as being more than just assessment results and that there is important data for school improvement in pupils' work in the broadest sense as well as in teachers' plans. He raises an important series of questions for teachers and managers when dealing with data and emphasizes the importance of preparation for its consideration. These are considered in more detail in one of the examples offered in Part 3, which provides illustrations of ways in which the ideas discussed in this part have been put into action.

3   Evidence-based Management in Action

In this part we present examples of evidence-based management in action. The case examples included here are based upon actual practice in primary schools.

We begin by setting out our ideas about how to manage the use of evidence. In particular, we concentrate on what we have learned about teachers' reactions to data. We argue that teachers need to be prepared to use data. Preparation includes helping teachers understand the validity of the data. It also involves preparing staff to deal with their emotional responses to findings. We suggest there are four responses teachers make to data. If a positive and constructive reaction is to be achieved, the process of analysing and reflecting on data collected has to be skilfully managed. If it is not, then it is unlikely that any subsequent action and improvement will follow.

The next section looks at using pupil perception data. We are committed to the idea of listening to what pupils have to say about their schools. Primary school children's perceptions of learning are formative in shaping their achievements, thus it follows that it is important to take such perceptions into account on a regular, systematic basis. Moreover, experience shows that this information is of great interest to teachers and other members of staff. Pupils' perceptions can make a useful starting point in using data.

The rest of Part 3 is devoted to four case examples. The first one looks at how a school used school-based enquiry to follow up an Ofsted inspection of the school. The second example describes how the headteacher of a primary school examined the school's internal capacity to improve and worked on developing shared leadership. The third example reports on a school's efforts to monitor the quality of teaching and develop greater consistency among the teaching staff. The fourth example focuses on managing school-based enquiry. The school reported on here used a combination of audit, review, staff development time and pupils' assessment data to establish an evidence-based approach to school improvement.

Together these four case examples illustrate how a sample of schools used some of the techniques described in Part 2. They also show how senior staff managed the process.

How to Manage Using Evidence in Schools: Teachers' Responses to Data

One of the major developments that has taken place in education during the last few years has been a considerable increase in the production of evidence about children's progress. As Southworth (1997, p. 2) has argued.

> Pupil data now plays a central part in informing a school's improvement efforts and this trend is set to continue and develop as target setting becomes one of the major initiatives in the next few years to raise standards of educational achievement.

Paying attention to pupil data has become a central element of national policy and a means of attempting to improve standards nationally. However, there is evidence to suggest that unless attention is paid to the development of the skills of analysis and interpretation, the aspirations and expectations of central government may flounder. In the early stages of the EPSI (The Essex Primary School Improvement) project, which was founded on the belief that teachers and governors of self managing schools should adopt a data driven approach to developing their schools, Southworth and his colleagues identified four major issues related to teachers' responses to data.

- Generally, there was a positive response from headteachers and teachers to using an evidence based approach to school development.
- Analysis and understanding data are presenting new challenges for heads and teachers.
- Pupil perception data is especially interesting and a stimulus for reflection amongst teachers.
- Links between the analysis and reflection on data and the implications for changes in teaching are presently relatively weak.

If schools are to achieve the improvements the staff want and children have a right to experience, it is fundamentally important that teachers develop an understanding of data and its analysis and more importantly are able to identify the most appropriate teaching implications that arise. As was explained in the last section, this was the subject of an investigation by Dudley (1999), who argued that there are three issues that need to be addressed if the proposed improvements in standards are to be achieved.

First, there is a need to change perceptions of what is meant by the term 'data' and to widen views of what is meant by 'performance data'. Data is a word with which many teachers feel uncomfortable, seeing it as primarily concerned with numbers and statistics.

> We need to build a recognition that data exist in many forms and that pupils' work and teachers' plans are 'data' and just as important in the picture of school and pupil performance as numbers or charts generated from surveys or assessment results. (Dudley, 1999)

This means that thought needs to be given to how both quantitative and qualitative data are to be used in the accountability process. Primary schools have relied heavily in the past on descriptions of achievement rather than numerical indicators. Both have their place but each of them have to demonstrate evidence of 'reliability' (Can I be sure that this result will be repeatable?) and 'validity' (Can I be confident that this assessment is a fair reflection of what has been taught?).

Second, in the management of the use of data within schools, it is important to understand the psychological reactions of teachers and how its analysis affects their actions and motivations. The existence of data does not always lead to action. Sometimes it is because the data are viewed as not being valid. Published tables of 'raw' results are dismissed by many as being unfair, whereas 'value-added' analyses appear to have been more successful. Since they focus on pupil progress, schools with difficult contexts can have their achievements recognized. This provides an illustration of the power that data can have when it is linked to an equally powerful psychology:

> Value-added data enjoy this validity and currency almost entirely because of psychologically *affective* factors such as trust and perceived fairness. They are clearly important ingredients in any data set intended to bring about changes in teaching strategies. (Dudley, 1999)

If teachers trust the results and accept the findings as a fair reflection of reality, it is more likely that analysis and findings will be acted upon.

Third, in the analysis, presentation and discussion of data effective management strategies need to be developed which prepare colleagues for what is likely to emerge. In order to investigate this, Dudley studied the reactions of groups of teachers to pupil perception data in four primary schools. The data were presented in the format illustrated in Part 2, as comparative responses by the children to the same questions from the Learning Perception survey. Four different response patterns were identified:

(i)   An active critical acceptance of the issue in the data was characterized by consideration, debate and reflection by the teachers on what the implications of the results might mean and a suggestion for action related to the identified concern.

(ii) A passive uncritical acceptance of an issue was demonstrated when teachers just accepted the information without reflection, debate or question.

(iii) A passive uncritical rejection of the data was typified by a tendency to generalize or rationalize the idea behind the data.

(iv) An active critical rejection of issues represented by the data was demonstrated when teachers scrutinized the data and explored reasons for the children's responses as determinedly as occurred with an action response before the issue was rejected or dismissed as being irrelevant.

The analysis of the teachers' responses revealed that an active response is slightly more likely to occur when the analysis presents positive information about a school's practice. Usually, however, when a response is positive it tends to be mentally 'filed away' but not challenged or reflected upon. When the response is predictably critical the findings are often likely to be ignored and not acted upon. Dudley suggests that it is not natural for schools to look for criticisms, but if schools are to improve, critical examination of successes, of what seems to work, must become as common as what seems to be going wrong. He argues that effort needs to be invested in preparing the ground for staff discussion of the analysis of data and suggests that teachers and managers should consider the following questions as a precursor to any discussion of data findings:

- What aspects of these data are particularly important for the school?
- What aspects of these data are particularly important for me?
- Ideally what would I expect the outcome to be?
- Realistically, what do I expect the outcome to be?
- What change or improvement strategies can we identify in advance of the discussion in order to promote positive action and avoid the negative effects of criticism?
- Have we safeguarded against making assumptions about home background and taken steps to challenge such assumptions when they arise?

Finally, Dudley suggests that most discussion about data has tended to be about the past, a reflection on results, rather than consideration of analyses that might influence the future. The introduction of target-setting has introduced a new form of data, data which focuses on the future, what the children might achieve. It has to be recognized that we are in the early stages of developing our expertise in this area and, as Hewett (1999) has argued, target-setting needs to be placed in the context of wider school improvement initiatives. As was suggested in Part 2, Hewett emphasizes that, in athletics terms, making significant, sound, sustainable educational progress is more like being a long distance runner than a sprinter. Success in target-setting should therefore be judged by how close a school gets to its targets rather than an expectation of always achieving or exceeding them. It is important for success to be judged against the previous achievement of a particular group for whom the target has been set rather than past year groups. The most difficult task is not how to set targets, but how to bring about the intended improvement.

Dudley concludes by arguing that the success of target-setting as an improvement strategy is entirely dependent on developing a positive attitude amongst teachers towards data and its analysis. In support of this, Southworth (1997) comments,

> The research skills of collecting and analysing quantitative data, and of developing interpretations or speculating about possible meanings, are not skills which heads and teachers feel greatly confident about. There may well be a good case for teachers being offered professional development opportunities in research skills. (p. 8)

Using the skills of school-based enquiry which require preparation, analysis and reflection before judgment should be a contribution towards the development of these skills.

The Pupils' Perspective in School-based Enquiries

In recent years, the educational press and a growing number of research projects have emphasized the importance of pupil attitudes and perceptions for improving the effectiveness of schools. For example, an editorial in the *Times Educational Supplement* (5 December 1997) argued that schools should 'Take children's views more seriously' and suggested that in future adults in general, and schools in particular, will have to take children's views much more seriously than they do at present. Ruddock (1996) has contributed much to our understanding of the importance of the student voice in school improvement in the United

Kingdom. She has argued that what pupils say about teaching, learning and schooling is not only worth listening to but that it provides important, perhaps the most important, foundation for thinking about ways of improving schools. Research in the Improving School Effectiveness Project (ISEP), using a pupil questionnaire (MacBeath and Mortimore, 1994), indicates that the items relating to the 'learner's engagement with school' and the 'learner's self-esteem' appear to have potential as important dimensions affecting achievement. In 1994, Michael Barber argued that, 'If more teachers are to succeed in unlocking the potential of young people . . . then issues of attitude, motivation, pupil self-esteem and peer group culture must take centre stage' (p. 5).

We have found in our work with primary teachers that even the youngest children are able to offer thoughtful and reflective reactions about their experience of school. For example, a 6-year-old offered the following comments about what makes a school effective.

- The children's work should be good.
- The teacher doesn't give work to the children which is too easy or too difficult.
- It shouldn't be the same work that all the children in the class do at the same time.
- Children shouldn't have races in their work.
- The children should do lots of different kinds of work.
- The teacher should show the children things, not just tell them.
- The whole school should meet and do things together so they can make friends.
- Children shouldn't fight at break times.
- There should be lots of books in the school.
- There should be places in the school where the children can read quietly.
- There should be pictures, paintings and sewing that the children have done on the walls.
- The children should be able to make things.

All of these expectations can be related to elements in the research into the effectiveness of schools. In the light of evidence of this kind, Ruddock et al. (1996) suggest,

> The history of reform in education . . . is of change efforts that are only partially successful because they fail to grapple with the deep structures of schooling. . . . We would argue that one of the weaknesses of reform efforts – and we have had our fair share of them – is

that they have persistently neglected an important dimension of the situation. If we are to be confident that the vast majority of young people will commit themselves to learning . . . then we have to take seriously young people's accounts and evaluations of teaching and learning and schooling. (pp. 177–78)

In a useful review of the research associated with the involvement of pupils, Pickering (1997) suggests there are six major reasons which justify the inclusion of the pupils' perspective in school-based investigations.

1 Putting pupils at the centre of their learning increases motivation.
2 Children's views on the progress of their own learning are helpful to teachers in planning their work.
3 The fact that it is 'their learning' that is in question entitles them to a significant degree of involvement.
4 Pupils can often contribute to the collection of evidence related to the improvement of teaching and learning. After all, it is something that is done to them! (Whereas, perhaps, it should be something that is done with them.)
5 The increasing levels of maturity demonstrated outside of school should be reflected, if not matched, in an appropriate way within school.
6 Finally, that if schools are to retain pupils, an issue facing an increasing number of schools, then teachers need to work with and reflect upon the world of children and consider its implications for the organization of learning within them.

In their longitudinal study of children's experience of the National Curriculum at Key Stage 1, Pollard and Filer (1996) observed that:

Young children become effective learners when their self-confidence is high, the classroom social context poses manageable risks and they receive sufficient, appropriate instruction and support. (p. 311)

A range of studies indicate that the influence of affective factors on children's learning is profound (Sylva, 1994; Raban-Bisby, 1995). From an early age children develop self-concepts of a mastery orientation or a failure orientation that have a major impact on later achievement or failure. As a learner it raises questions about whether I can expect to feel confident as I approach new learning. Am I likely to be supported in my learning and can I take risks and learn from mistakes? Or am I likely to be placed in a potentially negative learning situation where I have a fear of failure? The work of Dweck (1986) illustrates the differences between learners in this context. In her work, a distinction is made between positive and negative approaches to learning. Positive attitudes are evidenced by a belief that effort leads to success, an acceptance of one's ability to improve and learn, a preference for challenging tasks, and satisfaction from completing difficult tasks. Those who adopt a negative orientation believe that success is related to ability, satisfaction is gained from doing better than others, and there is a tendency to evaluate oneself negatively when the task is too difficult. An assumption of 'learned helplessness' can become established where any success is attributed to luck rather than effort or competence. Careful assessment enables the teacher to identify children adopting either of these reactions and to modify teaching accordingly.

A number of writers have argued that overcoming learned helplessness is dependent upon children understanding what is expected of them and the ability of teachers to identify children presenting these differing characteristics so that they can provide appropriate support. Dudley (1999) believes that if primary school children's perceptions of learning play an important role in their day-to-day achievement and are formative in shaping subsequent achievement, it follows that it is important to take such perceptions into account on a regular systematic basis. He goes on to suggest that the need to find ways of capturing perceptions is inescapable if we are to engage in improving learning. By exploring perceptions we begin to see the surface features of the attitudes beneath them. Pupil attitude surveys have consistently emerged as a means of doing this.

In a study of pupils' perceptions using a pupil attitude survey, Dudley argues that the affective elements of education are vital to the processes of learning and achievement and that we ignore paying attention to the pupils' perspective at our peril. He describes the structure and organization of the Learning Perception survey (What I like about school) which has been employed in the Essex Primary School Improvement Initiative (details of the questionnaire are included in Part 2, page 73). This particular questionnaire aims to explore children's views of six areas which research has suggested influence learning (i.e. the pupil's view of themselves as a learner; the learner's understanding of the purpose of learning and the effectiveness of feedback strategies employed by teachers; relationships with the teacher and the role of the teacher in learning; the pupil's perception of home/school relationships and involvement of parents in learning; pupil perceptions of peer group commitment to learning; perceptions of future achievement).

Dudley found that even the youngest pupils hold a range of established views about their learning and that clear gender differences became apparent. Boys were only more positive than girls on two items of the 25-item questionnaire. Boys tended to feel less positive than girls about access to teacher help, about how interesting they found their work and about how fairly justice is administered. Dudley admits that the items are prescribed and the responses closed, reducing the power of the survey to generate discussion beyond responding to statistics; however, involvement in the survey raised some interesting debates amongst teachers. Those who participated in his study found the presentation of results for children in their school as compared with other schools fascinating and established for many of them a wish to enquire further, especially into the issues behind children's responses, ways in which the information could be used to improve opportunities for learning and to influence the children's attitudes to learning. (An example of the analysis of the results for one of the questions which was used for discussion with teachers can be seen in Figure 3.1). Teachers responded to the data in a variety of ways, but it led a number of schools

to add to their list of management check points following any agreed policy change not only: 'How will this be viewed by the staff and by parents?' but also now, 'How will this be perceived by pupils?' (Dudley, 1996a)

The availability of comparative data proved to be a useful stimulus for discussion and to further enquiries by teachers into practice in their school and classrooms. Dudley also commented that gathering pupil perceptions can be eye-opening and supportive, but that it is important to remember that it can also be 'bruising'. Children can often be extremely frank and candid in their reactions. Dudley asks

Are you ready for what the data might bring? Are you going to give it the weight that it deserves or are you going to deny the data that does not fit with your perceptions? How will you resolve such dilemmas?

Dudley suggests that one way of developing the use of pupil data is to involve the pupils themselves as participant researchers in data gathering and analysis. As Fielding (1998) has so coherently argued

To exclude young people from the process of consultation is . . . foolish and frequently rests on an outmoded view of childhood which ignores

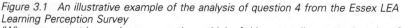

Figure 3.1   An illustrative example of the analysis of question 4 from the Essex LEA Learning Perception Survey
'When you are at home do you sometimes think of things to tell your teacher about?'

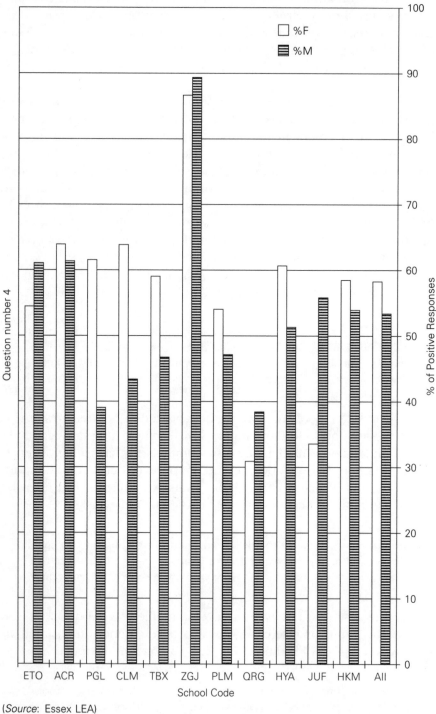

young people's capacity to reflect on matters that are of central concern to their lives. (p. 10)

The evidence presented here suggests that asking pupils for their opinions can be an interesting and productive way of starting a school-based investigation and can raise important issues for the improvement of practice especially if the focus is on the quality of teaching and learning.

Example 1: A School-based Investigation Following an Ofsted Inspection as Part of a Post Inspection Action Plan

This case study of River Walk 5–9 First School followed the inspection of the school by the Office for Standards in Education. In the report of this inspection, a number of concerns were expressed regarding the organization, structure and management of the curriculum at Key Stage 2. In particular, the key issues for action stated that:

- The organization for the delivery of the curriculum at Key Stage 2 needed to be reviewed in order to extend learning opportunities for some pupils.
- Steps needed to be taken to raise standards for some of the more able pupils in some subjects.
- Recognition needed to be given to the fact that learning is more effective when timetabling arrangements enable children to develop and discuss their ideas and when children are given opportunities to complete tasks.
- More able pupils should be given opportunities to pursue and sustain work at greater depth.

It was argued in the report that opportunities were limited by current time-tabling arrangements and there was further concern that insufficient attention was being given to planning for continuity and progression. It was accepted, however, that many of the concerns raised only applied to a minority of pupils and to a limited range of subjects at Key Stage 2.

Not surprisingly, such comments were of significant concern to the teachers working in Key Stage 2. They had invested a great deal of time, energy and personal commitment to creating a structure which related to many of the suggested weaknesses of the primary curriculum. In particular, that increased specialization for teachers and pupils, especially at the upper end of the primary stage, contributed to improvements in the quality of teaching and of standards of achievement (Ofsted, 1995; Ofsted, 1994; Alexander, et al., 1992). The school concerned had established a structure, where for two days each week the 8–9-year-old children worked a carousel of lessons which placed them with a 'specialist' for a half a day at a time. The remaining three days of each week was spent with their class teacher. The four teachers who taught the 8–9-year-old classes offered there own specialism as part of the programme so that the children experienced mathematics, physical education, information technology and science within the carousel of specialist teaching. The Ofsted inspection team were clearly concerned that such practice might be inappropriate for younger children in Key Stage 2, which is interesting given that standards were identified as exceeding national expectations in several subjects, notably Science, Music and Physical Education, which were a direct result of using the teacher expertise available at Key Stage 2.

The headteacher regarded the analysis of these concerns as being too sensitive to manage internally, so she invited an external consultant to provide an independent review of curriculum organization at Key Stage 2 and to offer recommendations for action in response to the issues raised in the Ofsted report. In order to gather evidence for this, the external consultant, a qualified Ofsted inspector, spent one and a half days in the school. Half a day was involved in reviewing curriculum documentation and a full day was spent using the skills of school-based enquiry, observing the Key Stage 2 curriculum in action and interviewing teachers, non-teaching assistants and children working in the Key Stage 2 area who were asked to explain and comment on their experience and perception of the organization.

It is important to recognize that one day spent observing in a school provides insufficient evidence upon which to make generalizable claims. However, some of the concerns expressed in the Ofsted report were confirmed but, in general, there was a great deal to commend in the organization which was in place. The report that was produced following an analysis of the data provided an indication of the progress that had taken place since the visit of the inspection team. During the day, children were observed engaged in Design/Technology, Mathematics, Science, Art, Information Technology, Music and Physical Education (Dance and Athletics). What follows is a synopsis of the report that was presented to the school related to the identified focus.

Issues that Emerged

- The organizational structure of the curriculum at Key Stage 2 is complex and it took some time for an outsider to understand the intricacies of the system.
- Nevertheless, all of the teachers who were invited to comment spoke enthusiastically about the system. They recognized that there were advantages and disadvantages but that, on balance, the advantages far outweighed the disadvantages.
- Every child who was questioned about their experience was able to explain clearly what they were doing, why they were doing it and how it related to previous activities in their programme. They spoke with enthusiasm about their experiences and particularly enjoyed the opportunity to work with other children and with different teachers for part of the week. It is important to remember that for a large proportion of the week, children are with their class teacher. Comments from the children included;

> 'I like working in this way. It gets boring working with the same teacher all of the time. Seeing different teachers is much more interesting.'

> 'I like having different teachers. I really like doing different things. It makes you feel older, more grown up.'

- This last comment was supported by the teacher who taught the class of children who would be joining Key Stage 2 in September. It was suggested that it was important that the children saw themselves 'progressing through the school' and that there was a need for a change in organization for the children to feel that they were 'growing up'. To that end, consideration had been given to developing a simplified version of the system for a part of their week during their final term in Key Stage 1. This was a most useful contribution to the development of continuity and progression throughout the school.
- One classroom assistant, whose children had experienced the system, spoke positively about it and argued that it had been invaluable preparation for the middle school. She suggested that the structure helped the children 'to develop independence and a sense of responsibility'.

- Another teacher, relatively new to the system, supported this. Although she accepted that she looked forward to the days when she was with her own class, she recognized that this was not necessarily true of the children who, over the year, 'gained in independence and were generally very responsible'.
- During the observations, there was evidence that opportunities were provided for children to achieve well above national expectations. This was especially true in Science and Physical Education (Dance).
- There was evidence that children experienced a variety of teaching and learning situations, including whole-class teaching, half-class teaching, whole-class discussion, small group work, working as pairs and working as individuals. There were occasions where appropriate tasks had been provided for children and some opportunity for children to take some control and responsibility for their learning.
- One great advantage of the flexibility that such a system presents is that it enables small groups of children to work with teachers who have expertise and enthusiasm for a particular area of the curriculum and for more regular interaction between teacher and children. This was certainly true in the context of information technology, where the children had access to a computer with programs appropriately matched to their level of ability and a teacher with an interest in that area. It was also evidenced in an art activity where the children were able to produce some quality printing because they had the easily available support of the teacher responsible for this area.
- There was an occasion, however, where children were introduced to an activity and left to follow it through on their own without sufficient understanding of what was expected of them. In this context, the children either did not know what to do or misunderstood the task and initially tackled it incorrectly. This only occurred on one occasion and as a result of two different curriculum areas of a very different nature being addressed in the same room. One group was involved in a maths activity and the other in a design technology activity. As soon as the teacher realized that there was a misunderstanding it was quickly rectified and the task clarified for the children. In the maths activity during this session, careful thought had been given to the differentiation of the task for children of differing levels of ability.
- There was some evidence to support the Ofsted claim that opportunity for sustained engagement in tasks was curtailed

for some children by the timetable structure. It was not possible for a group of children to complete a mapping activity, which would not be picked up again for several days. This raises a concern about the extent to which young children can easily return to a task they have left for some time. One teacher argued for the advantages of this, however, suggesting that they return to it with renewed interest after a gap. One of the observations illustrates this. In a very well organized science activity, the children spent time collecting evidence from the school grounds of insect and animal life. The children were thoroughly involved in the activity and there was effective use of questioning on the part of the teacher, who used questions to probe and extend children's understanding and to focus their observations. The teacher suggested that to have immediately turned to reviewing what had been observed would have meant having to reduce the time for data collection and, perhaps, some enthusiasm for the task. It was suggested that reflecting on their observations the next time they met would be seen by the children as a new activity and a further motivation for them. There was other evidence to suggest that the children were able to do this. In a Design/Technology activity, two children used ideas introduced the previous term to plan for the construction of joints for their fictitious animal, stimulated by the poem 'Jabberwocky'. They were able to explain in detail what they were doing, why they were doing it and where their ideas had come from.

- There was evidence of teachers linking aspects of children's curriculum experiences effectively, whilst at the same time staying within the context of specific subjects. For example, a poem studied as an English activity had served as a stimulus for a Design activity and was also used in an excellent Dance lesson. The standards of achievement presented during this session were considerably beyond those achieved by many much older children. Similarly, in the Music lesson observed an opportunity was taken to extend children's knowledge of places in the world and as a result reinforced recent geographical experiences.

- One final observation related to the use of parent helpers. In the afternoon a thoroughly well planned set of activities had been arranged for children to compete against themselves in a variety of athletics activities. The children were in groups, one with the teacher, another with a trainee teacher and two groups with parents. Whilst recognizing that we are always grateful for parental help and support, the differences in the children's experience were quite marked. Both teachers used praise and encouragement to motivate the children. They also used teaching points to help them improve their performance. One parent, despite trying very hard and with great enthusiasm, was spending most of the time disciplining and controlling the children and applying inconsistent standards of judgment to the children's achievements.

In the light of the investigation, a number of suggestions for improvement were offered:

- The documentation explaining and justifying the curriculum organization at Key Stage 2 needed clarification. The inclusion of illustrations of what was meant in practice would help others to understand the intentions and process more quickly. This would be beneficial for parents, governors, newly appointed teachers, teachers in training at the school, supply teachers and possibly for the children themselves.
- In some circumstances, thought needed to be given to the purposes and expectations of tasks set for the children. This was especially true when activities involving more than one subject area were planned and the children required to take some responsibility for themselves whilst the teacher is working with another group. Learning intentions need to be framed in terms of clearly expressed learning objectives which the children also understand.
- Further thought needs to be given to the timescale associated with particular tasks such that it is possible for some activities to be completed within the available time, whilst others may be carried over until a later time. This might involve introducing flexibility into the timetable to reflect the activities that are proposed. Consideration of the time needed for tasks then becomes an important feature of the planning process.
- Opportunities to develop parent support skills would improve the quality of provision and perhaps improve their satisfaction in the support that they offer to the school.

Governors at the school received the report positively and the teachers responded enthusiastically. As a result, a new brochure was produced that explained the aims and structure of the system. This has subsequently been used to induct new members of staff, as an explanation to parents, and a version has been produced for the children. Further consideration was also given to preparing parents for supporting activities in school.

This case study provides a useful example of how the employment of an external consultant and the skills of school based inquiry can clarify a situation and offer positive suggestions for improvement.

Example 2: Monitoring and Developing a School's Capacity to Manage Change

Park Street Primary School is situated in a large conurbation. It is located in a densely populated area, with most of the children living in owner-occupied terraced houses or rented tower block accommodation. There are 315 pupils in the school, 20 per cent of whom are eligible for free school meals. The school is housed in a 100-year-old building. However, the site and fabric of the building have always been well maintained and the school is in a very good state of repair.

The headteacher has been in post for seven years. The first five years of her headship were very intense. Many of the school's systems and structures had needed 'modernizing', almost all of the teaching staff changed, two moving on for promotion and all of the others retiring. Three years ago the school was inspected by Ofsted. The inspectors judged the school to be sound, but the staff were disappointed that the school was not rated higher. The teachers felt they had put a lot of effort into improving the school and thought the inspectors had not given them enough credit for moving the school on as much as they had.

After the inspection the staff had put together an action plan and had worked through all the key issues identified by the inspectors. They had also implemented the National Literacy Strategy and the Numeracy Strategy. All the teachers were now familiar with the literacy and numeracy hours. However, the headteacher believed that the staff had managed these changes in a rather mechanical fashion. They were not as enthusiastic as they had been before the inspection.

The headteacher had recently embarked on a higher degree course at the local university. She was studying for an MEd and had completed two modules. One of these had introduced her to the idea that as schools work on their improvement priorities they simultaneously need to create the in-school conditions and capacity to manage these intended changes. Reflecting on this idea the head began to recognize that she had been putting most of her energy into determining what needed changing, rather than how to implement the changes and how to sustain them once they were in place.

The headteacher therefore decided that there was a good case for developing the school's internal capacity to improve. In particular, the headteacher thought it would help the staff if they were to now begin to learn from each other rather more than they had in the past. The teachers continued to teach in relative isolation from one another and, apart from some infrequent classroom visits and monitoring by curriculum coordinators, the teachers were unfamiliar with one another's practices.

The head decided to use the Monitoring School Conditions questionnaire (Questionnaire 6 in Part 2; *see* page 70). She had come across this questionnaire on her Masters course when she read about the Improving the Quality of Education for All (IQEA) project (Ainscow et al., 1994). The questionnaire seeks the views of teachers, support staff and/or governors on six in-school conditions:

1 enquiry and reflection
2 planning
3 involvement
4 staff development
5 coordination
6 leadership

The questionnaire also enables those who administer it to use it to track, over time, how each of these six conditions is developing. Therefore, the headteacher decided to ask the teachers to complete it in July with the intention of re-administering it the following July when, hopefully, after a year's effort there would be signs of some of the six conditions developing.

Being unaccustomed to the questionnaire, the head decided that she would only use it with the teaching staff. Once she had become more familiar with it she could then begin to use it with support staff, governors and parents.

The head explained her thinking at a staff meeting and showed colleagues copies of the questionnaire. The teachers agreed to complete the questionnaires and accepted that the head should collect them in and analyse them. However, two teachers were concerned about confidentiality. They noted that the head would be able to detect who had said what. To overcome this problem and to ensure anonymity the teachers agreed to complete the questionnaire using the school's standard ball-point pens with black ink and to putting a ring around their response ratings. In this way no one could be identified by their favoured writing instrument or by their handwriting style!

Staff agreed to a deadline for completing the questionnaire and, rather than hand them in personally to the headteacher, a 'post box' in the secretary's office was created. Once all the questionnaires were filled in, the head spent an evening collating the results. These showed that staff thought that the planning, involvement and coordination conditions were fine, but that there was scope for more enquiry and reflection and staff development.

However, the major surprise for the head was the mis-match in her rating for the leadership condition and those of the staff. The head had responded to the four questions by rating them either 'often' or 'nearly always'. By contrast, the teachers were saying that there was rarely, or only sometimes, a clear vision, delegation, senior staff taking a lead and staff being given opportunities to take on leadership roles.

This finding perturbed the head and she discussed it with the deputy and another senior colleague. While they reassured her that the staff respected her and valued her strong and deep commitment to the school, they also said that the teachers were now ready to play a greater role in leading aspects of the school's development. Reflecting on this discussion and the questionnaire results the head realized that having appointed relatively inexperienced teachers four years ago she had been too protective of them for too long. They had matured and many of the teachers were now ready for additional challenges, responsibilities and opportunities.

During the summer recess the head reflected further on the findings. In early September she discussed first with the deputy and then the teaching staff an idea she had developed. Following these discussions it was agreed that, as part of the school's improvement plan for the new academic year, they would focus on how staff were teaching during the literacy hour. While some staff had also wanted to focus on the numeracy hour, it was eventually decided that it would be best to concentrate on one thing rather than two and, given that staff were now more familiar with the literacy period, it was right and proper to review it. The English coordinator was assigned responsibility for monitoring the hour. Of course, the English coordinator had already done some of this monitoring, but it was agreed that a more systematic approach was now needed.

The headteacher was able to buy in some supply teaching cover for the English coordinator to release her to visit classrooms and the head also 'topped up' this money by covering the class herself.

The English coordinator visited each of the other classes and observed them during a literacy hour. She drew upon the school's English policy and the teaching policy and the National Literacy Strategy documentation. The headteacher also arranged for the coordinator to meet an LEA Inspector to learn from him how Ofsted inspectors were looking at the literacy hour during an inspection.

Following these visits, which were all planned so staff knew when the coordinator would be in the classroom, the coordinator met each teacher individually to discuss what she had seen.

The English coordinator's literacy hour was observed by the deputy head, using the same approach and focus as the coordinator had adopted. With this external perspective of her own teaching and her first-hand knowledge of her colleague's teaching the coordinator compiled a report of the literacy hour. She had also undertaken to interview a sample of children from each class about their reading and she included their views in her report.

At the January staff development day the coordinator took the first part of the morning to present her views. The staff were greatly interested in what she had to say. The emerging picture was as follows: while all staff had implemented the hour successfully and felt it had made a positive difference to the children's reading skills and progress, the coordinator was struck by how much variation there was between the teachers. She had explored this further by looking at teachers' plans and by talking with the headteacher. This additional information largely confirmed her first impression that there was some inconsistency between teachers. These were more than individual teacher differences and could not be explained simply by differences in emphasis in the two key stages. Indeed, in two cases there were greater differences in teachers' approaches within a key stage than between teachers in Key Stages 1 and 2.

The pupil perspective data also threw up something new. The children all saw reading as something they did in order to be able to do their school work. No child, however, had said unsolicitedly that they saw reading as a pleasurable activity. This was strongly at odds with one of the objectives in the school's English policy which was to foster within pupils a 'love of literature.'

The staff were impressed by the coordinator's report. She had not identified any individual teacher and had focused on whole-school issues. The report was thorough and detailed. She had logged examples of what she had observed, including how each teacher had organized her/his classroom for reading. The report was challenging, even hard-hitting, but fair. While some staff were initially defensive, after a session when key stage staff discussed the report they all appreciated there were things to address.

During the afternoon session of the development day, the key stage teams were invited to set out what they thought should now be done. In the final session of the day these were shared and the head summed up the position. The head then said she, the deputy and the English coordinator would reflect on all that had been said and proposed and come to the next staff meeting with some ideas about how to move forward.

At the next staff meeting, the English coordinator proposed a plan of action. During the present term eight of the ten staff meetings which were planned would be devoted to looking, in turn, at how each teacher organized the reading materials in their classrooms. These staff meetings would be held in the teachers' classrooms. Also, school assemblies would be planned to include a wide range of stories and would include the promotion of literature and story-telling. Staff would also do the same in their individual classrooms. More displays of books, including recently purchased texts, would be mounted around the school. During the summer term a similar number of staff meetings would be devoted to teachers each reporting to the staff group how they were presently operating during the literacy hour, to identifying their strengths and their development needs.

This plan of action was agreed and implemented. The visits and meetings went well. Indeed, there were many benefits. As a result of staff meetings being held in classrooms more informal inter-staff visiting started. This was particularly noticeable between teachers in the different key stages. Previously these had worked as two rather independent teams, with little contact between years 2 and 3 and children in the Reception class and year 6.

In July the head re-administered the Monitoring School Conditions questionnaires. To her relief, staff were much more positive, particularly in terms of staff development, enquiry and reflection and leadership. The process of focusing on the literacy hour had proved beneficial, not least because of the contribution of the English coordinator, whose role was also seen by many staff as a symbol of delegated leadership. As one teacher wrote at the end of her questionnaire: 'I hope this year's work will now be followed up by a similar focus on the numeracy hour.'

Example 3: Monitoring Teaching

Primrose Hill Primary School is situated in a rural location, five miles outside the county town. Much of the employment provided in the town centres on administrative and clerical work, or is provided by the university. The village where the school is located has grown over the last decade and the school has increased in size accordingly. It is a popular school, with some children coming to the school from other villages and a few even travelling out of the town to attend. There are now 175 children in the school, with two classes housed in temporary classrooms. Some 25 per cent of pupils are eligible for free school meals and the children come from a wide range of social and economic backgrounds.

A recent Ofsted inspection was critical of the lack of consistency in teaching. This judgment was a surprise to many of the teaching staff, but not to the headteacher who had just arrived at the school a few weeks prior to the inspection. One of the features of the school which the head had noted was a lack of professional interaction between teachers. They were a friendly group, having worked together for over ten years. There had been no changes in the staff group. Socially the teachers got on well with one another, but there was little professional talk in the staff room. Staff meetings rarely became active discussions. This lack of interaction also meant there had been very limited visiting of classrooms. The monitoring that took place in the school consisted of subject managers looking at samples of pupils' work and reading teachers' plans. No formal observation of classroom practice took place, except by the headteacher, something the inspectors had also remarked on and identified as a key issue.

The *post*-Ofsted action plan stated that classroom monitoring would be introduced and that consistency in teaching would be addressed. The headteacher began by putting in place a policy for teaching and for learning. The process of compiling these policies was carefully designed in order that, at every step along the way, staff were involved and able to appreciate the implications of what was being introduced.

Staff development days had been devoted to examining what educational research shows about effective teaching. A lecturer from the local university's School of Education had led one of these days and also shared with the teachers recent thinking on the competencies expected and demanded of beginning teachers during their teacher training. These helped the staff to identify the specific skills they needed to be effective.

Staff had next moved on to agreeing their own 'ground rules' for teaching at Primrose Hill School. These included devising a 'lesson template'. This was a list of 'dos and don'ts' for teachers in terms of pre-lesson preparation, pupil entrance to the classroom, beginning the lesson, implementation of the lesson, ending the lesson. Staff adopted this style of planning, along with a more precise use of lesson objectives. They shifted from stating what they and the children would do to now specifying the intended learning outcomes for each lesson.

The headteacher monitored all of these developments by visiting every teacher's classroom and observing how they were implementing these new practices. As staff settled into these new ways the head suggested that they should now begin to visit one another in order to learn how they were each progressing. The head proposed a series of visits, with every teacher visiting one other colleague and being visited themselves, once every half-term.

While staff had been very comfortable with the head visiting them, there was some resistance to the idea of peer observation. This was eventually overcome by the head suggesting that the first round of classroom visits should be seen as introductory. Staff could then identify the lessons they needed to heed when setting up subsequent visits. The suggestion was accepted by the staff and the first round of visits commenced. These went well. Staff found them very valuable. They recognized that watching another teacher at work was professionally rewarding and valuable.

The headteacher created the time for these visits by covering classes herself. This was a heavy demand on her time, but she was able to monitor the classes' progress while teaching them and could gain some insights into each teacher's ways of managing the children and the classroom. Although the head had to postpone some of her administrative work, she found that by covering the classes she was able to continue her own monitoring role.

As time went by, the head was able to observe that consistency amongst the teachers was developing. When staff reflected on this they also believed there was greater consistency in their approaches to teaching. They attributed this to the new policy for teaching and to the lesson template.

When the time came for the third set of classroom visits the staff decided to take a specific focus. Until then they had been looking in a general way at teaching and learning. Now it was agreed to all focus on the same thing. After much discussion, at a protracted staff meeting one Monday evening, it was decided that they would look at teachers' questioning skills. As with previous visits they would work in pairs, each observing one another. They would feed back to one another but, given the agreement to all focus on questioning, it was decided that they would also share their reflections and thinking at a staff meeting.

The visits went ahead and went well. Much informal discussion was generated and it was quickly apparent to the head that the teachers were learning new things and being challenged by looking at colleagues' practice. One reason why the exercise was proving so developmental was the insistence of the headteacher that during feedback between the pairs they had to address two issues:

1   The observer had to say what s/he had observed. This then invariably led to a discussion between the observer and the observed teacher about what had taken place, why these things had happened and how successful the lesson and the teaching had been.
2   What the observer had learned about or was now thinking about her/his teaching in the light of what they had witnessed. This focus stimulated a lot of reflection and analysis of practice because it encouraged teachers to be professional learners and it did not imply that improvement of one's practice was a remedial activity, but a developmental one for all staff.

When the time came for staff to share what they had discovered from observing one another's questioning skills it emerged that the teachers had seen a great deal. One pair reported that one of them had used questions to very good effect during circle time. One such session a week was reserved for the teacher to explore through questions and answers that the children had learned that week in numeracy and literacy. Another pair had realized that they each varied the amount of 'wait time' they gave to the children. One of them only allowed the children 3 or 4 seconds to answer a question, while the other gave children 10 to 15 seconds. Moreover, the one who gave most time for children to frame their answers taught an older group of pupils. These findings had given the pair much food for thought and they triggered a lot of staff discussion.

Another pair of teachers in Key Stage 1 had discovered that one of them actually spent time helping the children to develop the capacity to ask questions themselves. The 5-year-olds played games to identify each other, discussed what constitutes a question and identified questions in written texts. They also used circle time to find out things about classmates and asked questions of visitors and classmates in a structured discussion time. All of this had emerged by chance when the observing teacher was informally 'interviewed' by a small group of children eager to ask questions of the visitor!

This staff meeting was followed up by two more which explored in greater depth the range of approaches to questioning and answering which had been identified from this monitoring exercise. It was agreed that each teacher would present a brief description of her or his approach to questioning so that the full range of strategies in use across the school could be audited and discussed. After this had been completed the deputy suggested that a more common approach to questioning be adopted by the staff. The deputy, in the light of what had been reported, set out a first draft of 'Practical Guidance for Teachers' Use of Questions'. This was reviewed by a working group of three staff, revised and presented to the whole staff. Further suggestions were noted, including the need to prepare children to ask questions themselves and to develop their answering skills. When the third draft of guidance notes was presented it was accepted and adopted.

The head has subsequently monitored their implementation in use in classrooms. Not only had the teachers put the ideas into practice, but there was also greater consistency in their approaches, particularly within key stage teams. As a result of all this work the head learned that monitoring can be professionally developmental. More than anything the headteacher now believes that peer observation of teaching and learning, when coupled with carefully managed feedback and follow-up meetings, are processes that lie at the heart of school improvement.

Example 4: Managing School-based Enquiry

King's Down is a large primary school with 465 pupils on roll. The headteacher of the school had been in post for four terms when he decided that a more evidence-based approach to the school's improvement was necessary. While he had attended to numerous aspects of the school during that time, the major tasks he had conducted were the appointment of a deputy head, the creation of a senior management team, and a detailed audit and evaluation of the quality of teaching and learning.

The audit of teaching and learning produced evidence of quite a lot of pupil under-achievement, particularly in Key Stage 2. For example, while children's achievements as measured by the SATs at the end of Key Stage 1 were in line with national and the LEA's averages, those at the end of Key Stage 2 fell below them. Also, from comparing the results at King's Down school with other similar schools, it seemed that apart from reading, pupils' learning outcomes were generally lower than in almost all the other schools.

In addition, his monitoring of the quality of teaching showed that in some classes expectations of children's work were not high enough. Standards were often satisfactory but children were not being pushed on as much as the head thought they should. This was particularly true in terms of years 3 and 4 and one class in year 5. When he taught these classes he found that the children, particularly the more able ones in English and mathematics, were able to achieve more than their class teachers demanded of them.

The head believed there were several reasons for this under-achievement. Many of the teachers had not taught in other schools either at all, or for a long time, and so had little awareness of standards in other schools. The children, coming from relatively advantaged homes, achieved satisfactory standards in English and mathematics quite com-fortably. However, too few pupils achieved the higher levels in their SAT results. Some of the teaching in years 3, 4 and 5 was worksheet-based and unchallenging. Also, there was a lack of differentiation in the teaching. This was particularly true for the more able pupils. When teachers differentiated they tended to focus on those children who were seen to be below average, rather than those who were average or above this level. Indeed, the head had recently come to question the notion of 'average' his teacher colleagues used. He believed the teachers used this term to mean 'children who are doing well enough'. Con-sequently, it made some colleagues unaware of those children who were capable of doing much better. This was compounded by the teachers' judging children's abilities only by reference to their language skills. If children could read competently, speak confidently, were articulate and could write fluently and accurately then the teachers judged them to be capable learners. There was little attention to how the children were doing in other subject areas, particularly those subjects not assessed at the end of the key stages.

When the newly appointed deputy took up her post the head asked her to conduct her own audit of the school. By the end of her first term the deputy broadly confirmed the head's view. These percep-tions were then shared with the senior management team (SMT). This team consisted of the head, deputy and two key stage leaders. The key stage leaders were surprised by the head and deputy's views. The Key Stage 2 leader was particularly concerned. However, over the course of the next three meetings the head shared with the SMT the pupil out-come data over the previous three years and related this to LEA informa-tion. Although both key stage leaders were sceptical of the accuracy of the SAT information they eventually acknowledged there were issues which needed exploring.

The head and deputy also learned from this experience. They now knew that using data with the staff was not going to be problem-free. They would have to take them through the data sets carefully and try to

avoid staff becoming so defensive that data analysis created professional paralysis.

The head and deputy decided that at the September staff development day they would each present to the staff their views from their
respective audits. After they had each presented their views the two
key stage team leaders would be asked to comment. Following these
presentations, the teachers would then divide into key stage groups.
The head would join the Key Stage 2 group and the deputy the Key
Stage 1 group. The two key stage leaders would conduct the meetings.
Staff would first be invited to each offer their reflections and then they
would examine for themselves the most recent assessment data on
pupils. These data included end of key stage results for the last three
years, year 4 data from QCA, reading test results and the NFER non-
verbal intelligence test data.

After lunch the key stage teams were each asked to report back
their interpretations of the data and asked to offer some action points
for the future.

The day proved to be remarkably successful, although parts of
the morning were uncomfortable for some staff and the headteacher
because the discussion became both over-heated and confrontational.
However, the head was able to convince everyone that the day was not
about finding culprits, but to do with trying to see what the children
were actually achieving compared to what everyone thought they were
accomplishing.

During the day the head realized that he had made a mistake. He
now felt it would have been better to have presented the data to the
staff for them to examine first, and then for their analyses of them to be
compared with the head's and deputy's interpretations. Organizing the
day the way he had, created a sense of 'us and them' and probably
contributed to the ensuing confrontation.

A major outcome from the day was the stated wish for staff to be
kept informed in much greater detail about pupils' assessment results
across the whole school, rather than just their own class and year group.
Also, staff wanted staff meeting time and at least one staff development
day a year to be used in analysing pupil data. The head agreed with
these ideas.

Many of the teachers also wanted to be involved in auditing pupils'
progress. The head agreed with this in theory, but asked staff to consider the time constraints. He suggested that the SMT should take overall responsibility for monitoring progress, involving subject coordinators
when appropriate. This was only partially accepted by the staff. Later the
head revised his position and said that each year all subject coordinators

should formally report to the SMT on pupils' progress in their respective subject areas, across the school. Also, these reports would be minuted and a written report prepared by the coordinator for presentation to the governor's curriculum committee.

The other major success the head detected during this development day was the way teachers were talking about pupils' progress. Formerly they had only ever mentioned pupils' attainments, but the data had also asked them to look at how the children were doing over time and to see how much progress the children were making. This had been picked up by the staff who quickly began to use progress as the key criterion of their success.

Although the head felt the day had introduced an evidence-based approach to pupils' performance, he now knew he had to build on this and firmly establish and sustain this approach. During the school year he made sure that coordinators played a part in monitoring pupils' progress. They were asked to look at samples of pupils' work and compare them with previous year's efforts. They also contrasted them with work stored in pupils' assessment portfolios, which were a form of records of achievement. In this way qualitative and quantitative information was used to gauge how pupils were doing.

At staff meetings during the Autumn and Spring terms the SMT organized analyses of pupil data. These were sharply focused discussions, looking at just one aspect of the pupils' learning. For example, at a meeting in November staff looked at pupils' spelling scores and compared them with their reading ages. They looked at similarities and differences in the results of boys and girls and trends in year cohorts. A good deal of preliminary work had been done by the SMT who were able, with the help of computer software, to present these data in tabular form so that staff did not waste time collating the data, but used all the available time to analyse them. One finding was that a significant number of the boys and a smaller number of girls who were deemed to be competent readers were relatively poor spellers. Several 'theories' were advanced as to why this was the case, so the English coordinator said she would contact a reading centre she had once visited and make some enquiries.

During January the Key Stage 1 staff began to predict how pupils presently in year 1 would perform when assessed at the end of year 2. This led to much inter-staff discussion and some debate. The head and deputy attended this meeting and were delighted at the quality of the discussion because some of the long-standing attitudes and expectations of the teachers were being set aside. This was evident when, having listed how each child was expected to do, the key stage leader asked everyone to now focus on the children again and suggest how they might be moved on through better support so their achievements could be enhanced. Many of the children predicted to gain a level 2 were identified as being capable of level 3 or 4 if they were given specific help and targeted support.

Colleagues in Key Stage 2 also undertook a similar exercise. They predicted how pupils in year 3 would score in year 4, and those in year 5 would achieve when in year 6.

These activities and the ensuing discussions raised particular lines of enquiry. For example, when staff made their predictions for pupils they soon moved into asking the question:

How might we stretch the more able?

In turn, this led them to consider:

What changes might we make to ensure that these pupils make better progress?

As the head noted, such questions were not being asked twelve months previously.

There were also several other benefits. Staff in Key Stage 2 began to review their lesson plans to see whether they were setting appropriate challenges and demands on groups of pupils. In effect, differentiation had begun to happen without the head or deputy having to appeal for it.

When the following September development day came around, time was again devoted to analysing the recent SAT results. One thing noted was that year 4 appeared to be a particularly strong cohort. They had scored higher than all other year groups in mathematics and reading, but not in science. This was a puzzle and the science coordinator was asked to review this and to monitor their progress, with their class teachers in year 5, during the next term.

Reflecting on the twelve-month period since an evidence-based approach had been introduced that involved all the teachers, the headteacher saw several valuable developments had taken place. First, old attitudes had begun to change. Staff were much more questioning of their own work and of the pupils' achievements. Second, a more differentiated view of pupils was emerging. Third, staff had begun to have a wider view of the school, as well as of their class, year group and key stage. Fourth, teachers were focusing on pupils' progress and beginning to examine whether children might be expected to do better and make greater progress. Fifth, the teaching staff were becoming more open

when they looked at performance data. They were now far less defensive than when they started and were willing to look at their teaching
and the pupils' learning from a variety of standpoints.

Overall, the staff had begun to be critical of their own and the
pupils' efforts. They were now debating ideas and findings identified in
the data, were reflecting on their insights and interpretations and developing an action orientation to these discussions.

The last point was especially important. This head had previously
been a head in another school. The staff at his former school had
developed an evidence-based approach, but he felt too much of the
staff's work in this area generated a lot of discussion but too little
action. He had been pleasantly surprised that the staff at King's Down
not only wanted to discuss pupil performance data, but also wanted to
try to do something about improving the children's progress. When he
considered why this had come about he believed the SMT had played
an important role in this respect. By collating data sets for the staff and
by looking at specific issues the staff had been able to focus directly on
something, rather than trying to look at everything or feeling free to
talk about anything. This also had the effect of ensuring there was
always time towards the end of each discussion when staff could attend
to the action steps they now needed to take. Sometimes these were to
collect more data, but often it was to set in motion a revised approach
to planning, pupil assessment, or teaching.

The head also recognized that it was usually the deputy who asked
the staff to consider what they should now do in the light of the evidence they had been discussing. The deputy was always keen to move
the discussion on from reflection to action.

Conclusions

Throughout this book we have made the case for evidence-based management and leadership. Knowledge of what is happening inside classrooms is vital to the work of school leaders. Clearly, monitoring is a key part of finding out what is happening across a school. However, we have argued that monitoring should be seen as an integral part of school self-evaluation.

School self-evaluation today involves, much more than formerly, attention to both processes and outcomes. It is also more focused than formerly through the use of targets and quantitative and qualitative performance indicators. Moreover, evaluation is action-orientated. Evaluation is not simply about judging the success of what has been happening; it is also intended to determine the next course of action.

Given that LEAs are today providing support in inverse proportion to schools' success, then the majority of schools need to develop stronger systems of audit, review and evaluation than was previously required. Senior staff, indeed all staff should take responsibility for analysing the school's success and identifying areas for development.

In building the case for school self-evaluation, we have provided many examples of how staff in school can conduct audits and analyses of their work. The techniques we have focused on include:

- Observation
- Interviews
- Questionnaires
- Documentary analysis
- Using assessment data

Furthermore, we have included some examples of what and how schools are presently doing.

The way we have organized the book reflects our interest and experience in attending to both the principles and the practice of school self-evaluation. Hence, as the book develops, the discussion moves from the general to the particular.

The examples of schools' approaches to evidence-based improvement also point to an important theme. As teachers develop an analytic approach to their work and the pupils' learning, a particular school culture develops. One important aspect of this culture is that it is achievement-oriented. Another is that it is strongly concerned with teachers' professional learning.

There are signs that senior staff in schools with whom we are working are developing particularly powerful ways of conducting school-based enquiries, and are using the information they gather from these enquiries to enhance teacher reflection and to inform staff development.

When classroom-focused enquiries are tightly linked to teacher development, staff begin to create learning schools: that is, schools which are able to be self-managing, self-renewing and improving. Schools in which all members of staff develop and where their professional efforts and skills are continuously refined and enhanced.

The culture of a learning school supports strong ties between teachers. There are high levels of professional collaboration, a strong sense of interdependence, practical sharing and teamwork. Heads, deputies and senior staff are active participants in these teams and groups; they guide them and encourage others to lead them and they also model ways of working together and demonstrate that they value groups as well as individuals.

Heads and deputies therefore need to work at the social conditions and organizational structures in the school. They need to look at developing partnerships among teachers, encouraging pairs and trios of staff to meet and work together. They need to ensure that staff meetings are effective and efficiently managed. Importantly, they must use each of these forms of professional interaction to develop dialogues about teaching and learning.

Given the staff's willingness to work together, then this also helps staff to engage in a range of monitoring activities. Moreover, as teachers begin to observe aspects of their own and the children's work, where this is a positive activity, then monitoring itself contributes to strengthening the culture. The processes of collecting and analysing evidence are also the means for creating and sustaining a culture of professional learning and school growth.

There is, however, one particular feature which needs to be emphasized: namely, that there is a systematic approach to monitoring teaching. The quality of teaching in schools needs to be observed, discussed and developed. We say this not because the quality of teaching is poor, but because the challenge of teaching in a primary school today is great and teachers need to keep on developing themselves as teachers throughout their time in the profession. The notion of life-long learning is as relevant to teachers as to other learners.

Strengthening how we meet pupils' needs includes developing the quality of teaching. Self-managing and improving schools should be places where teachers individually and collaboratively develop and hone their skills as teachers. We will not develop self-improving schools unless improving teachers' classroom skills becomes a feature of them. Certainly some off-site work will be needed and in-service activities at local centres and universities ought to accompany much we have suggested. Indeed, if there is to be sophisticated and deep analysis of data collected in schools by staff groups, then there will need to be increased provision to support this work and to develop teachers' research skills. However, our main point here is to stress that unless and until enquiry and reflection include attention to pedagogy – to the classroom skills and practices of teachers – then school improvement will remain limited.

Attention to pedagogy involves looking at teaching. It means focusing on aspects of our teaching we are unsure about, want to understand better, or where we feel we lack some confidence. It means developing over time a repertoire of approaches and skills. It means trying out new forms and methods of teaching.

When there is a high level of attention paid to teaching this provides the basis for supporting teachers' growth as teachers. What we propose here is that we begin to develop pedagogy by design, inside the schools where we teach, as well as sometimes on courses elsewhere and sometimes supported in school by external agents.

We need to see our schools not only as places where we work and teach, but also as workplaces where we learn about our teaching with and from our colleague teachers. This means installing processes and procedures for teachers to talk about their teaching, for them to observe and be observed teaching, for feedback sessions to be conducted and for individual teacher development plans to be formulated which include attention to teaching skills and competencies. It also means mentoring one another and developing teacher 'buddy' schemes or partnerships. In small primary schools it may well involve pairing teachers from different schools. Some school clusters might introduce this regardless of school size.

Many of these forms of peer assistance have been hinted at in much of the foregoing. However, there is one element that has yet to be mentioned and that is coaching. In addition to all the different kinds of support which staff will need, they will also need some clear, explicit and targeted help. Probably the most beneficial way of providing this help is through coaching.

If a colleague has considerable knowledge, understanding and skill in the teaching of, say, reading, then surely it makes sense for that individual teacher to coach others who are less experienced, or less confident, or less skilled. In turn, those who are especially talented in teaching science, art or whatever can then play their part in coaching. Coaching means spreading the individual talents of a group of teachers to all so that we become as a team of teachers greater than the sum of our parts.

Coaching also means encouraging teachers to do more of what they already do well, namely teaching. Coaching in this sense means teaching a colleague or group of colleagues about something you do well. It is teachers teaching teachers.

Where these four sets of ideas, about culture, monitoring, pedagogy and coaching are implemented then staff in these schools will have established an evidence-based approach to their teaching, to the pupils' learning and to their own professional learning. We will have teachers who are researching their own professional practice and developing and sharing their craft knowledge and wisdom. Moreover, they will be committed to continuous improvement and to their own life-long professional learning. They will also have created by themselves and for themselves a learning school.

Learning schools have long interested us as an idea. However, the evidence-based approach we have advocated in this book actually tran-scends the notion of learning schools. Self-improving schools, which use evaluation to identify areas for development and which attend to the quality of teaching and teachers' pedagogic development, are *learning and teaching schools*.

In learning and teaching schools staff look closely and continu-ously at the pupils' learning – their outcomes, gains and progress. The teachers also use these data to examine their teaching. They observe one another's teaching and use this information as the basis for strengthening and developing their teaching skills and repertoires. In particular, teachers support one another in practical ways. They share their expertise and experience; they talk about their classroom practice and they offer one another practical help. In such schools teachers grow. They become better teachers, not by accident but in a coordinated way that is orchestrated and led by senior staff.

An evidence-based approach to school improvement plays a major role in creating the conditions for staff to transform their workplaces into learning and teaching schools.

References

ABERCROMBIE, M. L. J. (1969) *The Anatomy of Judgement*, Harmondsworth: Penguin Books.

ACHESON, K. and GALL, M. (1980) *Techniques in the Clinical Supervision of Teachers*, New York: Longman.

AINSCOW, M., HARGREAVES, D., HOPKINS, D., BALSHAW, M. and BLACK-HAWKINS, K. (1994) *Mapping Change in Schools: The Cambridge Manual of Research Techniques*, Cambridge: University of Cambridge Institute of Education.

AINSCOW, M., HOPKINS, D., SOUTHWORTH, G. and WEST, M. (1994) *Creating the Conditions for School Improvement*, London: Fulton.

ALEXANDER, R. (1985) *Primary Teaching*, London: Holt, Rinehart and Winston.

ALEXANDER, R., ROSE, J. and WOODHEAD, C. (1992) *Curriculum Organisation and Practice in Primary Schools: A Discussion Paper*. London: DES.

ASHTON, P., HUNT, P., JONES, P. and WATSON, Y. (1981) *The Curriculum in Action*, Course PE 234, Milton Keynes: Open University Press.

ASSOCIATION OF ADVISERS AND INSPECTORS FOR ASSESSMENT (London Branch) (1998) *Setting Targets for Pupils' Learning and Attainment*, London: AAIA.

BARBER, M. (1994) *Young People and Their Attitudes to School: An Interim Report of a Research Project in the Centre for Successful Schools*, Keele: University of Keele.

BARBER, M., JOHNSON, M. and GOUGH, G. (1994) 'The twin towns project – Raising expectations and achievement in city schools: Community partnership to national strategy', Submission for the Queens Anniversary Prizes for Higher and Further Education, Keele University: Centre for Successful Schools.

BARRS, M., ELLIS, S., HESTER, H. and THOMAS, A. (1988) *The Primary Language Record Handbook*, London: ILEA/CLPE.

BARTH, R. (1990) *Improving Schools from Within: Teachers, Parents and Principals Can Make a Difference*, San Francisco: Jossey Bass.

BASSEY, M. (1995) *Creating Education Through Research: A Global Perspective of Educational Research for the 21st Century*, Kirklington Moor Press: BERA.

BELL, J. (1987) *Doing Your Research Project: A Guide for First-time Researchers in Education and Social Science*, Milton Keynes: Open University Press.

BELLON, J. J. and BELLON, E. C. (1982) *Classroom Supervision and Instructional Improvement: A Synergetic Process*, Dubuque: Kendall Hunt Publishing Company.

BERWICK, G. (1994) 'Factors which affect pupil achievement: The development of a whole school assessment programme and accounting for personal constructs of achievement', Unpublished PhD Thesis, Norwich: University of East Anglia.

BROWNING, L. et al. [undated] *Team-Based Action Research*, Ford Teaching Project, Cambridge: Cambridge Institute of Education, pp. 11–17.

BIRMINGHAM ADVISORY AND SUPPORT SERVICES (1997) *Standards in Primary Schools: Report to the DfEE on Birmingham LEA's School Improvement Planning Project 1996/97*, Birmingham: Birmingham City Council Education Department.

BIRMINGHAM LEA (1997) *Raising Standards in Primary Schools: Report to the DfEE on Birmingham LEA's School Improvement Planning Project 96/97*, Birmingham: Centre for School Improvement.

CARTER, K. and HALSALL, R. (1998) 'Teacher research for school improvement', in HALSALL, R. (ed.) *Teacher Research and School Improvement*, Buckingham: Open University Press.

COHEN, L. and MANION, L. (1985) *Research Methods in Education*, 2nd edition, London: Croom Helm.

CONNER, C. (1991) *Assessment and Testing in the Primary School*, Lewes: Falmer.

CONNER, C. (ed.) (1999) *Assessment in Action in the Primary School*, London: Falmer Press.

CONNER, C. and AINSCOW, M. (1990) *School-Based Inquiry: Notes and Background Reading*, Cambridge: Cambridge Institute of Education, mimeo.

CONNER, C., DUDLEY, P. and WILKINSON, K. (1998) *Analysis of the GEST School Effectiveness Special Projects (1b) 1996–97: A Report for the Department for Education and Employment*, Cambridge: University of Cambridge School of Education.

CROLL, P. (1986) *Systematic Classroom Observation*, London: Falmer Press.

DEAN, J. (1993) *Organising Learning in the Primary School*, 2nd edition, London: Routledge.

DfEE (1996) *Setting Targets to Raise Standards: A Survey of Good Practice*, London: HMSO.

DfEE (1997) *Excellence in Schools*, London: HMSO.

DfEE (1997b) *From Targets to Action: Guidance to Support Effective Target-setting in Schools*, London: DfEE.

DONALDSON, M. (1979) *Children's Minds*, London: Fontana Books.

DREVER, E. (1995) *Using Semi-Structured Interviews in Small-Scale Research: A Teacher's Guide*, Edinburgh: SCRE.

DRUMMOND, M. J. (1993) *Assessing Children's Learning*, London: Fulton.

DRUMMOND, M. J. and McLAUGHLIN, C. (1994) 'Teaching and learning – The fourth dimension', in BRADLEY, H., CONNER, C. and SOUTHWORTH, G. (eds) *Developing Teachers Developing Schools*, London: David Fulton.

DRUMMOND, M. J., ROUSE, D. and PUGH, G. (1992) *Making Assessment Work*, Nottingham: NES Arnold and The National Children's Bureau.

DRUMMOND, M. J., SHREEVE, A. and VOEGELI, I. (1994) *Asking Questions: Teachers, Children, Classrooms. Classroom Evaluation in Norfolk*, Norwich: Norfolk Educational Press.

DUDLEY, P. (1999) 'Using data to drive up standards: Statistics or psychology', in CONNER, C. (ed.) *Assessment in Action in the Primary School*, London: Falmer.

DUDLEY, P. (1999a) 'Do pupil perception surveys work with young children?', in CONNER, C. (ed.) *Assessment in Action in the Primary School*, London: Falmer Press.

DWECK, C. (1986) 'Motivational processes affecting learning', *American Psychologist*, Vol. 41, pp. 1041–1048.

ELLIOTT, J. (1991) *Action Research for Educational Change*, Milton Keynes: Open University Press.

ESSEX COUNTY COUNCIL LEARNING SERVICES (1997) *Setting and Achieving Challenging Targets at Key Stages 1 and 2: A Practical Guide for Senior Managers and Governors in Primary Schools*, Essex: Advisory and Inspection Service.

FIELDING, M. (1998) 'Students as researchers: From data source to significant voice', Paper presented to the 11th International Congress for School Effectiveness and Improvement, School of Education, University of Manchester, UK, 4–7 January.

FLANDERS, N. (1972) *Analysing Teaching Behaviour*, Reading, Mass.: Addison-Wesley.

FORSYTH, K. and WOOD, J. (undated) 'Ways of doing research in one's own classroom', booklet. *Ford Teaching Project*, Cambridge: Cambridge Institute of Education, pp. 14–15.

FOSTER, P. (1996) *Observing Schools: A Methodological Guide*, London: Falmer Press.

FULLAN, M. (1991) *The New Meaning of Educational Change*, London: Cassell.

FULLAN, M. (1993) *Change Forces*, London: Falmer.

GALTON, M. (1983) 'Searching for meaning', Open University Course E364, Curriculum Evaluation in Educational Institutions: Milton Keynes.

GALTON, M., SIMON, B. and CROLL, P. (eds) (1980) *Inside the Primary Classroom*, London: RKP.

GRIFFIN-BEALE, C. (ed.) (1984) *Christian Schiller: In His Own Words*, London: NAPE.

HALSALL, R. (ed.) (1998) *Teacher Research and School Improvement: Opening Doors from the Inside*, Buckingham: Open University Press.

HARGREAVES, D. H. (1992) 'The new professionalism', Paper presented to the Fourth International Symposium on Teacher's Learning and School Development, University of New England, New South Wales, July.

HARLEN, W. (1978) *Match and Mismatch*, Edinburgh: Oliver and Boyd.

HARLEN, W. (1985) *Primary Science Taking the Plunge: How to Teach Primary Science More Effectively*, London: Heinemann.

HEWETT, P. (1999) 'The role of target-setting in improvement at the Leys Primary School', in CONNER, C. (ed.), *Assessment in Action in the Primary School*, London: Falmer Press.

HITCHCOCK, G. and HUGHES, D. (1989) *Research and the Teacher: A Qualitative Introduction to School-Based Research*, London: Routledge.

HOLLY, P. and SOUTHWORTH, G. (1989) *The Developing School*, London: Falmer.

HOOK, C. (1985) *Studying Classrooms*, Deakin, Australia: Deakin University Press.

HOPKINS, D. (1985) *A Teacher's Guide to Classroom Research*, 1st edition, Milton Keynes: Open University Press.

HOPKINS, D. (1993) *A Teacher's Guide to Classroom Research*, 2nd edition, Milton Keynes: Open University Press.

HUBERMAN, M. and MILES, M. B. (1984) *Innovation Up Close*, New York: Plenum.

KEMMIS, S. and McTAGGART, R. (1988) *The Action Research Planner*, 3rd edition, Victoria: Deakin University Press.

LEWIS, A. (1992) 'Group child interviews as a research tool', *British Educational Research Journal*, 18 (4), pp. 413–421.

LEWIS, I. and MUNN, P. (1987) *So You Want to Do Research! A Guide for Teachers on How to Formulate Research Questions*, Scottish Council for Research in Education (SCRE), Practitioner Minipaper 2.

Loose, T. (1997) 'Creating a learning culture', in *Managing Schools Today*, May, pp. 33–35.

MacBeath, J. and Mortimore, P. (1994) *Improving School Effectiveness Project: Pupil Questionnaire*, Edinburgh: Scottish Office Education Department.

MacBeath, J., Boyd, B., Rand, J. and Bell, S. (1997) *Schools Speak for Themselves: Towards a Framework for Self-evaluation*, London: National Union of Teachers in association with the Quality in Education Centre University of Strathclyde.

McMahon, A., Bolam, R., Abbott, R. and Holly, P. (1984) *Guidelines for the Review and Internal Development of Schools, Primary School Handbook*, York: Longman.

Millett, A. (1998) 'Let's get pedagogical', in *Times Educational Supplement*, 12 June, p. 28.

Munn, P. and Driver, E. (1991) *Using Questionnaires in Small Scale Research: A Teacher's Guide*, Edinburgh: Scottish Council for Research in Education.

Newlands, P. (1985) 'Specialist teaching: Implications for practice in the primary and middle school', *Curriculum*, Vol. 6, No. 1, Spring.

Newson, J. and Newson, E. (1976) 'Parental roles and social contexts', in Shipman, M. D. (ed.) *The Organisational Impact of Social Research*, London: Routledge and Kegan Paul.

Ofsted (1994) *Primary Matters: A Discussion on Teaching and Learning in Primary Schools*, London: Office for Standards in Education.

Ofsted (1995) *The Annual Report of Her Majesty's Chief Inspector of Schools. Part 1: Standards and Quality in Education 1993/94*, London: HMSO.

Ofsted (1998) *School Evaluation Matters*, London: Ofsted.

Oppenheim, A. N. (1966) *Questionnaire Design and Attitude Measurement*, London: Heinemann.

Osborn, M. with Croll, P., Broadfoot, P., Pollard, A., McNess, E. and Triggs, P. (1997) 'Policy into practice: Creative mediation in the primary classroom', in Helsby, G. and McCulloch, G. (eds) *Teachers and the National Curriculum*, London: Falmer.

Pascale, C. (1990) *Managing on the Edge*, New York: Touchstone.

Perry, W. G. (1978) 'Sharing the costs of growth', in Parker, C. A. (ed.) *Encouraging Developments in College Students*, cited in Bassey, M. (1995) *Creating Education through Research*, Kirklington Moor Press, in conjunction with BERA.

Pfister, J. (1997) 'Evidence of value', in *Managing Schools Today*, September, pp. 22–25.

PICKERING, J. (1997) 'Involving pupils, SIN (School Improvement Network)', in *Research Matters*, No. 6, Spring, London: University of London Institute of Education.

POLLARD, A., BROADFOOT, P., CROLL, P., OSBORN, M. and ABBOTT, D. (1994) *Changing English Primary Schools*, London: Cassell.

POLLARD, A. with FILER, A. (1996) *The Social World of Children's Learning*, London: Cassell.

PRISK, T. (1987) 'Letting them get on with it: A study of unsupervised talk in an infant school', in POLLARD, A. (ed.) *Children and Their Primary Schools*, London: Falmer Press.

RABAN-BISBY, B. (1995) 'Early childhood years – Problem or resource?', *Dean's Lecture Series 1995*. The University of Melbourne.

ROSENHOLTZ, S. (1989) *Teachers' Workplace: The Social Organisation of Schools*, New York: Longman.

RUDDOCK, J., CHAPLAIN, R. and WALLACE, C. (1996) *School Improvement. What Can the Pupils Tell Us?*, London: Fulton.

SARASON, S. (1990) *The Predictable Failure of Educational Reform*, San Francisco: Jossey Bass.

SIMONS, H. (1987) *Getting to Know Schools in a Democracy*, Lewes: Falmer.

SIMPSON, M. and TUSON, J. (1995) *Using Observations in Small-scale Investigations: A Beginner's Guide*, Edinburgh: Scottish Council for Research in Education.

STENHOUSE, L. (1975) *An Introduction to Curriculum Research and Development*, London: Heinemann.

STIERER, B., DEVEREUX, J., GIFFORD, S., LAYCOCK, E. and YERBURY, J. (1993) *Profiling, Recording and Observing: A Resource Pack for the Early Years*, London: Routledge.

SOUTHWORTH, G. (1996) 'Improving primary schools: Shifting the emphasis and clarifying the focus', in *School Organisation*, 16 (3), pp. 263–280.

SOUTHWORTH, G. (1997) 'Emphasising evidence-based developments in teaching and learning in primary schools', Paper presented to the annual conference of the British Educational Research Association, University of York, September 1997.

SOUTHWORTH, G. (1998) *Leading Improving Primary Schools*, London: Falmer.

SOUTHWORTH, G. (1998a) 'The learning school: What does it look like?', in *Managing Schools Today*, January, pp. 29–30.

SOUTHWORTH, G. (1998b) 'Target setting', *Primary File*, Vol. 33, pp. 133–136.

STOLL, L. (1994) 'School effectiveness and school improvement: Voices from the field', in *School Effectiveness and School Improvement*, 5 (2), pp. 149–77.

STOLL, L. and FINK, D. (1996) *Changing Our Schools*, Buckingham: Open University Press.

SYLVA, K. (1994) 'The impact of early learning on children's later development' (4.1) in C. BALL (ed.) *Start Right: The Importance of Early Learning*, London: Royal Society of Arts.

SYLVA, K., ROY, C. and PAINTER, M. (1980) *Childwatching at Playgroup and Nursery School*, London: McIntyre.

TIMES EDUCATIONAL SUPPLEMENT (1997) 'Take children's views seriously', *TES*, 5 December, p. 20.

WALKER, R. (1985) *Doing Research. A Handbook for Teachers*, London: Methuen.

WALKER, R. and ADELMAN, C. (1975) *A Guide to Classroom Observation*, London: Methuen.

WEST, M. and HOPKINS, D. (1996) 'Reconceptualising school effectiveness and school improvement', Paper presented at the American Educational Research Association annual meeting, New York, University of Cambridge School of Education, mimeo.

YOUNGMAN, M. B. (1986) *Analysing Questionnaires*, University of Nottingham School of Education.

Index